CITY OF LIFE
CITY OF DEATH

My parents, Dietrich and Erna, 1938.

CITY OF LIFE
CITY OF DEATH

Memories of Riga

MAX MICHELSON

UNIVERSITY PRESS OF COLORADO

Published by the University Press of Colorado
5589 Arapahoe Avenue, Suite 206C
Boulder, Colorado 80303

The University Press of Colorado is a cooperative publishing enterprise supported, in part, by
Adams State College, Colorado State University, Fort Lewis College, Mesa State College, Metro-
politan State College of Denver, University of Colorado, University of Northern Colorado,
University of Southern Colorado, and Western State College of Colorado.

The paper used in this publication meets the minimum requirements of the American National
Standard for Information Sciences—Permanence of Paper for Printed Library Materials. ANSI
Z39.48-1992

Library of Congress Cataloging-in-Publication Data

Michelson, Max, 1924–
    City of life, city of death : memories of Riga / Max Michelson.
      p. cm.
    Includes bibliographical references.
    ISBN 0-87081-642-X (alk. paper)
    1. Michelson, Max, 1924– 2. Jews—Latvia—Rāga—Biography. 3. Holocaust, Jewish (1939–
1945)—Latvia—Rāga—Personal narratives. 4. Rāga (Latvia)—Biography. I. Title.

DS135.L33 M536 2000
940.53'18'092—dc21
[B]

                                                                        2001027210

Designed and typeset by Daniel Pratt

10   09   08   07   06   05   04   03   02   01   10   9   8   7   6   5   4   3   2   1

Excerpt from Oscar Handlin's "Introduction" in Simon Dubnov *History of the Jews,* copyright
1967 by A. S. Barnes and Co., Inc. Reprinted by permission of Julian Yosellof.

Excerpts from Anatol Lieven, *The Baltic Revolution,* copyright 1993 by Anatol Lieven, reprinted
by permission of the Yale University Press.

Excerpt from the Yom Kippur Memorial Service from Central Conference of American Rabbis,
Gates of Repentance, copyright CCAR, 1976. Reprinted by permission of Central Conference of
American Rabbis.

To my beloved grandchildren
Rebecca, Daniel, and Anna
and
In loving memory of
my son Gregory

Contents

Preface

I begin the story of my life with my childhood and teenage years, prior to the terrible events of World War II and the Holocaust. My sheltered and peaceful life was disrupted by the Soviet takeover of Latvia in July 1940 and was then irrevocably shattered by the nazi occupation of Riga in July 1941. Many of the people described in this memoir perished in the Holocaust, including my parents, our relatives and family friends who were in Riga at the outbreak of the war, and the majority of my own friends and classmates. It is disturbing to describe the events of long ago with a knowledge of what would happen later. It is particularly painful to write about my family members and friends, knowing the imminent brutal disruption of their lives.

Part I of these memoirs describes Jewish life in Riga in the early decades of the twentieth century and recalls the many who perished there at the hands of the Germans and Latvians. I seek to honor the victims by remembering them—they must not remain nameless. By evoking their memory I hope to give lasting testimony to their interrupted, unfinished lives.

Part II describes the fate of the Jews of Riga and my own experiences in the Riga Ghetto and concentration camps during the nazi years. In the ghetto and particularly in the concentration camps we had a circumscribed, limited perspective, deliberately constrained by our nazi jailers. This restricted view differs, naturally, from the more objective descriptions of these events that became available after the war. Also included are brief sketches of my relatives and friends who spent the war years in the Soviet Union and Western Europe.

Acknowledgments

This book grew out of the many talks describing my wartime experiences at schools, colleges, synagogues, and churches throughout the Boston area. I am indebted to the many friends and listeners who urged me to prepare a more thorough narrative of my war years, and I thank them for their encouragement and support.

Linda Greenwood, Tom Weil, and Sonya Weitz read earlier versions of the manuscript. Their constructive comments have provided a useful basis for further evolution of the book. Lengthy and repeated discussions with Bob Ditter and Elizabeth Bidinger on various aspects of the story have been exceptionally helpful. I thank Jeffrey Weiss for his generous help in preparing photos and maps.

My good friend Marilyn Harter has been most generous in her encouragement of my efforts, and her thoughtful comments have been invaluable. Marilyn's steadfast support greatly helped see this book through to completion.

I am particularly grateful to my son Gregory for the careful reading and long discussions of many versions of the manuscript. Gregory's astute comments helped me crystalize many important issues related to my experiences. His incisive questions, critiques, and thoughtful suggestions were of great use in the preparation of this book.

My cousin Zvi Griliches kindly shared his memories and photographs of our family, which have greatly enriched the story. We had complementary recollections, and I cherished our many conversations and discussions.

Thanks also to Alan Feldman, Sylvia Rothchild, and Phil Zuckerman for their advice and practical suggestions with regard to publishing this book. Nancy Witting's and Cheryl Carnahan's careful editing has been extremely helpful.

Last but not least, I thank my beloved wife, Julie, for her forbearance during the long years when I was often preoccupied with writing the memoirs. Julie was always supportive of this endeavor, always ready to read yet another draft chapter, and always willing to offer honest and constructive criticism of the work in progress. I am deeply grateful to her.

NOTE ADDED IN PUBLICATION

Our son Gregory died suddenly of an asthmatic attack in September 1999, and my cousin Zvi Griliches died of pancreatic cancer in November 1999. I loved them dearly and miss them terribly.

CITY OF LIFE
CITY OF DEATH

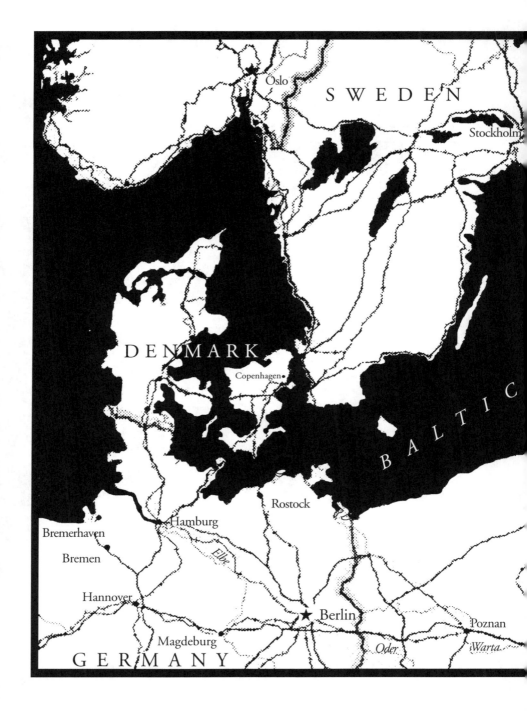

Baltic Sea region showin

PART I
Growing Up Jewish in Prewar Latvia

Forgetting is the Final Solution.
—THEO RICHMOND

#
My Background

I was born in Riga, Latvia, in 1924, the second child in an upper-middle-class Jewish family. My sister, Sylvia, eight years my senior, was born in Moscow. My parents had delayed having a second child because of the disruption of World War I, the family's evacuation to Moscow and eventual return to Riga, as well as the political uncertainties of the period. By the early 1920s the situation in the now independent Latvia had stabilized, and my family resumed a comfortable existence in the large villa adjoining our plywood factory. The household was ruled by a matriarch, my paternal grandmother Emma, with the help of our Latvian cook. My father, Dietrich (David), was born in 1879 in Riga, the oldest of five children; my mother, Erna Griliches, was born in 1890 in Vilna and was also one of five siblings. Her family operated a tannery in Dvinsk.

I grew up in a Jewish atmosphere, albeit one where religion did not play a central role. Orthodox Judaism, the only religious expression available, occupied a secondary position in our lives. Even as we acknowledged it as our religion, we considered it archaic, not relevant or essential to life in the twentieth century. At the same time, although dismissing religion from our daily existence, we decisively identified ourselves as Jews. Being Jewish was perceived largely in cultural and ethnic terms, and it found expression in a strong sense of belonging to one people. This identification was to some extent dictated and reinforced by the outside community, which classified everyone in the population in terms of their ethnic origin. Jews found this identification reasonably congenial and were comfortable with this arrangement. Jews also thought of themselves as a separate people and had very limited social interaction with the general community.

The problem of Jewish survival in a hostile Diaspora was widely debated. For many, Zionism provided a secular messianic solution to the so-called Jewish question, how to normalize the situation of the Jews in Eastern

Europe. We lived in a society that took anti-Semitism for granted but discounted its potential for large-scale violence and mayhem. Even the dramatic rise of Hitler and his explicitly anti-Semitic rantings did not warn us of the imminent catastrophe. In the nation-states of Europe, the Jew was the other, the perennial outsider. In times of economic hardship and depression he became a ready scapegoat. Rather than find effective solutions that would address and resolve the crisis, governments fanned the prevalent anti-Semitism by blaming the Jews for their difficulties. Anti-Semitism persists to this day, although virtually no Jews are living in the newly independent Latvia. Latvians are also blaming the local ethnic Russians for their problems. The Russians have taken the place formerly occupied by the Jews as a convenient scapegoat.

To me as a child, Latvia seemed safe and secure. Although I was well aware of the persecutions of the Jews, I believed they were ancient history, that the pogroms had occurred long ago and far away. Yet the history of Jewish settlement in Latvia is one of exploitation, persecution, and uncertainty. The concession of the right of Jews to reside in Riga to the subsequent extermination of the city's Jewish community took place in a span of only 100 years, about four generations. And those years were hardly a golden age. My childish belief that twentieth-century civilization had brought an end to persecution of the Jews now seems hopelessly naive, yet this belief was shared by many of my elders. When we recognized the danger posed by endemic anti-Semitism, it was already too late.

My paternal grandparents came from the western Latvian province of Courland (Kurzeme in Latvian),* which had been conquered and colonized by the Germans in the thirteenth century. German culture remained dominant in the area even after its annexation by Russia, and the German language was widely used. Jews were not permitted to settle in significant numbers in Courland until the seventeenth century. There were repeated expulsions that, however, were not rigidly or consistently enforced. Frequently, the threat of expulsion was simply a pretext for mulcting the Jews. Jews came north to Courland from Lithuania and Poland, where they had lived for several centuries. To a lesser extent they also reached the Courland ports of Libau (Liepaja) and Windau (Ventspils) from the Netherlands by way of Germany, in the wake of the expanding German Hansa trade along the Baltic Sea.

Jews worked as tax farmers, vodka distillers, innkeepers, small merchants, and peddlers. Generally, the only source of credit available to peasants

---

*Place-names in Latvia are frequently different in Latvian, German, and Russian. I have generally used the German (or in some cases the Yiddish) names for locations referred to prior to World War I and the Latvian names for places after the establishment of an independent Latvia in 1918.

was from Jewish pawnbrokers. Useful to the dukes and the landowning gentry as both creators and sources of wealth, the Jews were to some extent both protected and exploited by them. Townspeople—burghers, merchants, and artisans—unwilling to tolerate Jewish business rivals clamored incessantly for onerous measures intended to restrict the Jews' economic and social activities or for their outright expulsion from the province—something the German barons were loath to do.

After it came under Russian rule, Courland remained outside the Pale of Settlement—those provinces of Russia where the Tsarist authorities suffered Jews to reside. The Pale was intended to keep the newly acquired, large Jewish population out of the provinces of Russia proper. The Pale of Settlement was first established after 1772, the first partition of Poland. Following the liberalization under Tsar Alexander II, Jews belonging to several categories were permitted to live outside the Pale of Settlement. Among these were merchants of the First Guild, persons with higher educations, and, in some cases, artisans. In 1881, however, new limitations were again imposed on Jewish settlement outside the Pale. At the time, such restrictions were imposed not just on Jews but on all inhabitants of Russia.

Courland was briefly included in the Pale after 1795. Then, under Tsar Nicholas I the province was again removed from the Pale, although Jews who had previously been registered there were permitted to stay.[1] The prohibition on Jewish settlement was not stringently enforced, and significant numbers of Jewish residents always resided there. By 1850 the number of Jews in Courland had risen to 22,000, and by 1897 it had more than doubled to 51,000.[2]

In April 1915, during World War I, the Tsarist government ordered the expulsion of all Jews from the province of Courland. The government and the military leadership accused the Jews of treachery and scapegoated Jews for disastrous reverses suffered by the Russian army. The expulsion was brutally enforced. Almost 40,000 Jews were given one week to leave and were permitted to take only a few possessions. Most of the exiles did not return to their homes after the war, which effectively destroyed the thriving Jewish communities of Courland.[3]

Although the expulsion must have affected my paternal grandparents' families, I do not recall any discussion of these events in our home. The Jewish community of Riga had mounted a concerted relief effort, and our family must have been fully involved. My family avoided freely discussing unpleasant issues, and disturbing information was withheld from the children.

The expulsion decree did not apply to the Jews of Riga, as Riga was not part of Courland. As the German armies advanced toward Riga, however, my family also escaped to Moscow in the late fall of 1915.

2
Grandmother Emma

My paternal grandmother Emma—I called her *Omama* (the German intimate appellation for grandmother), or Oma for short—was the head of our household. Only in the early 1930s, when her health began to fail, did she relinquish her position. My bedroom was next to my grandmother's, and we spent many afternoons together there. It was a quiet and comfortable place, an escape from my outdoor games and sandlot soccer matches. I enjoyed being with her. I watched her play solitaire and cheat whenever an impasse occurred. Oma would teach me the game and let me help her play, or she would tell me stories of her childhood. She treated me to candies and chocolates, which I recall being particularly delicious.

Emma was born into a large well-to-do family in Frauenburg (Saldus in Latvian), on an estate leased and managed by her father. The estate, Sessilen, was owned by a Baltic German absentee landlord. According to my grandmother, her family enjoyed a grand manorial lifestyle; they often went on outings or visits to neighboring estates in a stately horse-drawn carriage. Emma was very proud of her father. She described him as an imposing, handsome man, and she held many fond memories of growing up on the estate he managed.

Emma's father, my great-grandfather Noah (Nikolai) Hirschfeld, was one of three brothers, all merchants, from Grobin, a small town near the Baltic port of Libau (Liepaja) in western Courland. Noah had twelve children, five sons and seven daughters, from two marriages. All of his children grew to adulthood, and all of them married. My grandmother told me that Noah's first wife, Emma's mother, Taube, had come from Holland. Emma was the next to last of her nine children. Taube died when Emma was about four.

Oma talked often about her sisters, four of whom where close to her in age. These sisters must have been very close as children. Emma was very fond of them, was in frequent correspondence and contact with them, and

The five youngest Hirschfeld sisters, ca. 1895. Left to right: Lina Herzberg, Emma Michelson, Minna Kretzer, Johanna Levensohn, Rosa Braude.

always referred to them as Tante Rosa, Tante Lina, Tante Johanna, and Tante Minna. My grandmother's stories gave me the impression that I knew them well, although they were scattered all over Europe, and Rosa was the only one I had actually met.

Emma mentioned her brothers less frequently. Four of them were considerably older than she, and all her brothers had died before World War I. They had all been merchants; two owned grocery stores in Frauenburg. The others also lived in the immediate area. They had raised large families, and the Hirschfeld clan was large and close-knit. My father, aunts, and uncles maintained intimate friendships with a number of the many cousins who were frequent visitors to our house. I addressed many of them as "uncle" or "aunt" but had difficulty understanding their exact relationship to us.

Emma and my grandfather Max (Mordechai) were married in Frauenburg in 1878. My grandfather Max, after whom I am named, died long before I was born. He was a manufacturer whose family originally came from Bauska in Courland. Max was born and educated in Mitau (Jelgava in Latvian), the provincial capital of Courland, 30 miles southwest of Riga. Like Grandmother Emma, Max also came from a large family; his father Solomon Michelsohn, a merchant, had nineteen children by two wives. Max was the fourth child and only son of the first wife, who died when he was very young. In 1856 Solomon married his second wife, Esther Hinda

My grandfather Max Michelsohn, ca. 1906.

Gordon, a woman age nineteen who bore him six boys and nine girls, two of whom died in infancy. It is perhaps not surprising that in the official rabbinic records Esther Hinda's cause of death at age seventy-four is listed as "exhaustion."

Solomon's sons attended the secular Mitau Realschule (high school), a German-language boys' school. In 1878 Solomon moved his family to Riga to participate in and benefit from the new economic opportunities there. Riga was at that time the largest and fastest-growing city in the Baltic area. Solomon's two youngest sons were the first members of the family to attend college, the Riga Polytechnic Institute.

I do not recall my grandmother Emma ever talking about her father-in-law, my great-grandfather Solomon. At home in our library hung pictures of a man and a woman dressed in the old-fashioned black garments traditionally worn by observant Jews of that era. I was told they were my great-grandparents, but I do not know whether they were on my grandfather's or my grandmother's side.

One of my granduncles, David, my grandfather Max's half-brother, was a dentist who ran an old-fashioned practice in Riga. I went to him until my early teens. He used an ancient foot-pedal–driven drill and generally took a very relaxed attitude toward dental problems. He was only ten years older than my father, but I thought of him as an old man, partly because of

My grandparents' family at home in Riga, ca. 1902. Left to right: Dietrich, Eduard, Clara, Tora, Max, Thea, Emma, Leo.

his antique office and partly because of his appearance. Other members of my family may also have been his patients, but to my knowledge we never met socially. Later, when I required orthodontic work, my parents blamed it on his neglect, and I started to see a more modern dentist.

My grandparents had five children; my father Dietrich (David) was the oldest, followed by Clara, Eduard, Leo, and Thea. The five siblings were very close and were genuinely devoted to each other, particularly Eduard, Clara, and Leo. My father, although supportive and concerned, remained more distant. My grandfather Max died unexpectedly at age fifty-seven in 1908; the cause of his death is unknown to me. After his father's death, Dietrich assumed the role of head of the family. As for Thea, the siblings loved and cared for her but treated her more like a child than an equal. Her mother Emma, in letters to her older daughter Clara, also referred to the adult Thea as "the dear child." Throughout her life Aunt Thea did retain a childlike quality, which made people want to take care of her.

The sheer volume of her surviving letters to Clara and Leo testifies to Emma's concern about the health and well-being of her offspring. Emma's children were polite, kind, considerate, and respectful to their mother, but except for Thea, they generally disregarded her suggestions and arranged their lives as they saw fit. Although her children's independent natures were trying, Emma nevertheless loved to be surrounded by her family. She viewed her children and grandchildren with great pride. My aunts and uncles visited Riga frequently, particularly during the summers when the family would rent a villa at Riga Beach (Jurmala), a favorite vacation spot. I remember her excited anticipation of seeing her children and her obvious joy when everybody had arrived. Emma also maintained close ties with her extended family; I remember frequent family gatherings with a large number of cousins in attendance. As might be expected, Emma was less close to her in-laws. We met socially with just a few of the relatives from my grandfather's side of the family.

Emma considered herself a Jewish aristocrat and felt her family held an exalted station in the community. She was a strong-willed person with an imperious manner. Genya Balson, the daughter of my mother's uncle Abram, told me she lived in Riga for six years in the early 1930s but never visited her cousin, my mother Erna, because she found my grandmother intimidating. In conversations Emma would refer to people as "he" or "she" or "that person," and we were expected to understand immediately to whom she was referring. If one failed to meet her expectations, she would become indignant and remonstrate: "Him. You know who I am talking about. You know him."

In her own way my grandmother was a religious woman. Even as she picked and chose what Jewish customs and traditions to follow, she identified herself strongly as a Jew. Shabbat candles were a Friday night fixture in our household; for many years I took them for granted without understanding that it was a religious ritual. Shabbat candles flickering in the early darkness of winter evenings evoke for me the peaceful and secure atmosphere of my childhood home. On Yom Kippur Emma spent the entire day at the synagogue, but if she ever set foot there at any other time I never knew of it. She did not keep kosher except during Pesach (Passover). Pork or shellfish was never served. Nonetheless, boiled ham or Canadian bacon occasionally appeared on our table, invariably accompanied by humorous but defensive comments referring to them as veal or turkey. My grandfather Max had probably been more observant than his wife, but I doubt that the household observed *kashruth* (Jewish dietary laws) during his lifetime. The only other religious symbol in our house was a *mezuzah* (a small case containing a prayer inscribed on parchment) on all doorposts. The *mezuzah* must have been attached when my grandparents first moved in but had not been looked after and had long since been painted over.

Like many Jews of Courland, my grandmother was influenced by German culture and was very outspoken in her admiration of everything German. Emma was well acquainted with German literature, poetry, and music. A family legend has it that during his stay in Riga, Richard Wagner was once a visitor in her home. Cultural alignment with Germany (as opposed to Russia) was typical of the Jews who were connected through service to the Baltic German gentry, often going back several generations. For Emma, as for many Jews, Germany represented emancipation—a window on Western culture and the modern world. The attitude of Latvians toward Germany was rather different; for them it denoted oppression, subjugation, and exploitation.

Emma was partial to blond hair and non-Semitic features. She described a child whose looks she found attractive by saying that he or she "does not look Jewish." My father and mother did not use that expression. Although Emma admired non-Jewish looks, she viewed conversion to Christianity with scorn. This attitude was shared by my family, including myself. Conversions were more prevalent in nineteenth-century Russia, where economic opportunities and advancement for Jews were severely circumscribed. When talking about Jews who had converted, my father would invariably mention that fact, using the derogatory Yiddish *geshmad* rather than the more neutral German *getauft* (baptized). Apostasy was a treacherous step, reflecting unscrupulous opportunism or extreme self-hatred; viewed with suspicion, converts were despised and often ostracized from Jewish society.

Although my mother came from a Russian-speaking family and my father and grandmother were both fluent in Russian, at home we spoke German. Except for communicating with our Latvian cook, Anna, who knew little Russian and no German, Latvian was not spoken in our home. Until the twentieth century Latvian was the language of peasants, not used by educated people. This attitude continued in Jewish circles even after 1918, when Latvia became an independent state. During my father's student years, Latvian was not taught at his high school or at Riga Polytechnic Institute. Nonetheless, both my father and Uncle Eduard had a good command of the language, because it was essential for dealing with workers at the factory and with the authorities. My mother's first language was Russian; in her native Dvinsk not only Jews but most of the non-Jewish population spoke Russian. My mother's Latvian was rudimentary, barely adequate for making purchases in shops and at the market.

The majority of the Jewish population of Courland and Riga spoke Yiddish, but my family did not consider Yiddish a language in its own right. They called it *Jargon*, implying that it was a corrupted German spoken by uncultured people who did not know "proper" German (i.e., Hochdeutsch, or High German). In our social circle its use was disparaged. It was not spoken in our home or by any of our relatives or friends.

Nevertheless, I suspect that most of my family members understood Yiddish and were more or less fluent in it. I do not believe Yiddish was spoken in my grandmother's home; all my grandmother's sisters whom I met spoke German. On the other hand, judging by the traditional Yiddish names of my paternal great-grandfather Solomon Michelson's children, Yiddish was likely spoken in his home. For Emma, Yiddish must have been an unwelcome reminder of the oppressive religiosity of her youth, from which she and her family had managed to escape, and was undoubtedly perceived as a threat of a return to an earlier, narrow-minded, and stifling society. Nonetheless, some Yiddish words found their way into even our home.

Unlike my family, I think of Yiddish as a beautiful and interesting language. I learned Yiddish in the ghetto and camps, where it was the lingua franca among Jewish inmates. There I met Jews from many different countries and heard a variety of Yiddish accents. In particular, it was a pleasure to hear the sounds of a pure Vilna Yiddish, a graceful and mellifluous language. To my amazement I also encountered Jews from parts of Hungary and from Greece who did not speak Yiddish. We were not able to communicate with each other. Although I am far from proficient, after the war I taught myself to read Yiddish. Based on an archaic German with a heavy admixture of words from Hebrew, Russian, and other origins, it is a separate language in its own right, not a corruption of present-day standard German. There has been a revival of interest in Yiddish in the United States in recent years. I am supporting the National Yiddish Book Center, which is preserving and distributing Yiddish books here.

My grandmother managed the household personally. With the help of our live-in cook, Anna Ulpe, she decided on the daily menu and, on important occasions and celebrations, helped with the cooking. Anna was a Latvian peasant girl who had an out-of-wedlock son. She had come to the city after her son was born. Anna had been with us for as long as I could remember and did not leave until 1940. Our house, together with the factory, was nationalized by the new communist regime, and we were no longer in a position to have servants.

Anna, a warm, earthy person in her middle thirties, had the plump appearance of a typical Latvian peasant: a round face, with full cheeks and a slightly bulbous nose. She wore her long, light brown hair in a tightly coiled bun at the back of her head and usually covered it with a kerchief. Anna could be relied upon to have definite, if not always rational, opinions about anything and anyone, which she was never shy about expressing. With time she became and acted almost like a member of our family. She had her favorites and not-so-favorites among our relatives and visitors and regularly commented to me about them. Particular targets of her resentment were occasional overnight guests who insisted on taking daily baths.

Anna declared that it was not healthy to bathe so often, that they risked scrubbing off their skin. She was probably more annoyed at having to make a fire in the wood-burning water heater in the bathroom and clean the bathtub after them.

Anna's domain was the kitchen and her bedroom, located directly off the kitchen. The kitchen was spacious and got plenty of sunlight, which made it very pleasant and bright during the day. After dark, however, it was dimly lit by a single bare lightbulb. Even by the standards of the day, it lacked modern conveniences. There was no running hot water, but squeezed into a corner was a small cold-water sink. Dishes had to be washed in a basin filled with hot water from the stove and then dried by hand.

The stove, a built-in, glazed brick wood-burning range, was the focal point of the kitchen. The stove had a small basin that provided a limited reserve of hot water, a roasting and baking oven, and a large warming oven used only for storage of pots and pans. The range top, a heavy cast-iron plate, had several openings whose size could be adjusted up or down by the addition of concentric, tight-fitting cast-iron rings. The rings could be removed to expose the pot to the desired level of heat from the flames and embers of the fire inside. Pots could also be heated indirectly on the hot cast-iron plate. The roasting and baking oven was built into the body of the range. The oven temperature could not be set but only coarsely controlled by changing the intensity of the fire inside the range.

The old musty-smelling icebox was almost never used. Perishable foods were kept on the windowsill in the pantry. When the weather was warm, Anna would shop daily in the market for whatever was needed. In the 1930s the markets in Latvia overflowed with dairy products, meats, fish, and poultry. The market in Riga was large. It was housed in four former airship hangars, one each devoted exclusively to meats, dairy, fish, and vegetables, respectively. There were also outside stalls for more vegetables, as well as many booths selling household goods and clothing. I revisited the market during my 1997 trip to Riga. Food is again plentiful, and everything is displayed openly and without refrigeration. In the meat pavilion, the sight of endless cuts of beef and pork, all uncovered, is enough to turn one into a vegetarian.

In my grandmother's considered and often pronounced judgment, her family's physical and spiritual health could best be sustained by good, plentiful, and nutritious food. She always saw to it that we had the best the rich Latvian Jewish cuisine had to offer. Butter, eggs, cream, and meats, the bountiful products of our local agriculture, were staples. Then as now, the ubiquitous ingredient in Latvian kitchens was sour cream, called *Schmand* in the Baltic German dialect. It is an especially rich and delicious product, hardly comparable to any sour cream available elsewhere. *Schmand* was justly famous throughout Europe, especially in Germany. It is the essential ingredient of many recipes. During my recent visit to an authentic Latvian restaurant in Riga, it was impossible to find a dish on the lengthy menu that did not use at least a dollop of *Schmand*.

Under my grandmother's tutelage, Anna had learned to cook the rich Jewish cuisine. After my grandmother's death, when Anna became the un-contested mistress of the kitchen, she continued in the same tradition. Not only was the food rich, Emma saw to it that everyone received generous portions as well as multiple helpings—seconds were obligatory, and it gave her special pleasure if we consented to a third helping. Large, multicourse meals were the focal point of our social gatherings; even informal afternoon teas never lacked a rich torte or pastry. Emma ran an open, hospitable house, and last-minute guests frequently joined us at our meals.

An inveterate manager of other people's lives, Emma tried to find rich matches for her poorer nieces. She was instrumental in arranging several marriages, but despite her tireless efforts the results tended to be unsatis-factory: the husbands were not young, they lost their fortunes during the war and the revolution, and they died, leaving destitute widows.

One of Emma's earliest and more successful matchmaking ventures involved her niece Charlotte (Lotte) Kretzer, the oldest child of Emma's older sister Minna. The two sisters had married within a year of each other, and both lived in Riga. Minna's husband, Elias Kretzer, died at forty-three, leaving Minna penniless, a widow of thirty-three with three small children: Lotte, age nine; Viktoria (Tora), eight; and Theodor (Fedya), three. My grandparents helped support her and treated her children like their own. Tora, a contemporary of my aunt Clara, came to live in my grandparents' home. Tante Minna died in the 1910s. Tora married a man from Odessa, and we lost contact with her in the early 1930s when she moved from Odessa to Moscow.

Minna's older daughter, Lotte, was thirty when Emma arranged a match between her and a prosperous Riga entrepreneur, Jakob Hirsch Kaplan, the owner of a flourishing cardboard factory. Kaplan, like my grandfather Max, was a merchant of the Second Guild. Under the Tsarist regime, Jews were not permitted to change their names from their original given Jewish ones. Accordingly, he is listed in the 1914 Riga City Directory as Yankel Hirsch Kaplan. The father of two teenage children from his first marriage, he was a self-made man from an impoverished background who had built up a substantial business. Jakob Kaplan was a renaissance man with wide-rang-ing eclectic interests—a brilliant but difficult and self-centered person. Lack-ing a formal education, he had read widely and had acquired an easy facil-ity with German and an impressive knowledge of German culture. He wrote in German—philosophical essays, poetry, and whimsical rhymes—which he published and presented to friends and relatives.

Jakob and Charlotte Kaplan's Silver Anniversary, 1933. My sister, Sylvia, is at bottom right.

Kaplan, though short of stature, had an imposing presence and spoke forcefully and with great authority. He was nine years older than my father and played the role of elder sage in our social circle. Kaplan loved to be asked his opinion and made weighty pronouncements on issues of the day. At festive family affairs he recited verses he composed in honor of the occasion while Lotte beamed with pride and admiration. She was fiercely protective of her husband. Their marriage, though childless, appeared to be a good one. It lasted until Kaplan's death from a stroke in 1940, during the Soviet occupation of Latvia. Lotte was killed the following year in the liquidation of the Riga Ghetto.

In 1918 Emma sat for a portrait by my uncle Leo. The painting, now at the Michelson Museum of Art in Marshall, Texas, shows a vibrant woman in her prime. By the early 1930s Emma was ailing. She sat for another portrait in 1933, which is still in my possession. The decline in her health was evident. She grew progressively weaker and died peacefully at home in January 1935. She was laid out in our large sitting room, and the funeral was postponed for several days to allow all her children to arrive from Western Europe. According to Jewish custom, the coffin had no lid but was covered with a dark blue cloth with an embroidered Magen David. Our entire family sat with her, and I felt a sense of peace and serenity in her

My grandmother Emma, ca. 1925.

presence. Our family observed the Jewish customs of mourning: *keriah,* cutting the mourner's garment at the cemetery, symbolizing the mourner tearing his or her clothing; and sitting shivah, seven days of mourning for the dead. During shivah the family again gathered in the large parlor and, sitting on the traditional low mourners' bench, received relatives and friends who came to pay their respects.

Emma was buried next to her husband, Max, in the Old Jewish Cemetery, which otherwise was no longer in use. During the German occupation of Riga, the cemetery became part of the Riga Ghetto and was desecrated and vandalized by the nazis.* Ultimately, after the war the Soviets removed the surrounding brick wall and what remained of the monuments and gravestones, and leveled the area. During my trip to Riga in 1996, I visited there and found that a small marker recalling the site of the former cemetery has been installed. Otherwise, there is no vestige of the Old Jewish Cemetery. It is just a neglected, overgrown wooded lot in an impoverished neighborhood.

---

*I lowercase "nazis" throughout because I do not feel they merit the respect of having their name capitalized.

3

The Jewish Community of Riga

Riga was part of the province of Livland, which was outside the Pale of Jewish Settlement. With a number of individual exceptions, Jews were not permitted to live there. Livland, originally named Livonia by the conquering German knights, was called Vidzeme after Latvian independence. At the beginning of the nineteenth century, a few Jews were granted the right to settle in Riga, and in 1842 the Jewish community was officially recognized. Gradually, more Jewish families moved there to share in the business opportunities offered by this burgeoning commercial center. The initiative and entrepreneurial spirit of the Jewish merchants and businessmen contributed significantly to the rapid growth and development of the local economy.

The Jewish population of Latvia expanded rapidly in the late nineteenth century. Just before the start of World War I, the number of Jews in the region peaked at about 185,000. The expulsion of the Jews from Courland in 1915 and the evacuation and flight into Russia during the war sharply reduced the number of Jews living in the area. In 1920 about 80,000 Jews were living in the newly independent Latvia. With the return of refugees from Russia, the number increased to 95,000 by 1925 and remained at that level during the 1930s. Jews constituted about 5 percent of the population of Latvia at that time.[4]

About half of Latvia's Jews lived in Riga. The city had only 25,000 Jewish inhabitants in 1920, but by 1939 that number had risen to 45,000—about 12 percent of the city's total population. Riga was an important center of trade between Russia and Western Europe. It was a cosmopolitan city that drew inspiration from the latest developments and ideas in Western Europe, particularly Germany. The city was also the heart of the country's Jewish cultural and political life.

Jewish entrepreneurs contributed significantly to the vitality and growth of the economy in Latvia during the period between the two world wars.

More than a quarter of Latvia's commercial enterprises employing ten or more people were owned by Jews. Jews dominated professional occupations, particularly as doctors, dentists, and lawyers. They were the intelligentsia: a well-educated, cultured, multilingual urban people. They read Jewish newspapers published in Yiddish and Russian. They went to Jewish theater. They read Jewish books—fiction, poetry, and philosophy—and produced a wide variety of Jewish artists. Oscar Handlin, in his introduction to Simon Dubnov's *History of the Jews,* described a view of Judaism shared by the majority of these intellectuals and professionals:

> Although Dubnov was a free thinker, he could not entirely detach himself from the Orthodox world of his forebears. He retained a high regard for the culture of the East European Jews, even though he felt he had grown beyond its religious origins. The need for reconciling his modern thinking with the inherited values of the group were basic to his distinctive form of nationalism.
>
> Dubnov expected that cultural nationalism would replace Orthodox religion as the cement that held the Jewish communities together. . . . He insisted that national identity was essentially cultural rather than political. The Jews were therefore a nation like any other, capable of leading an autonomous cultural life wherever they happened to be in the Diaspora.[5]

In the years immediately following World War I, organizations representing the entire Jewish political spectrum were active in Latvia: Marxists, communists, and socialists; Zionists and Revisionists. Endless discussions, disputes, squabbles, and fierce infighting among the different political factions were conspicuous in the Jewish scene in Riga. Zionism exerted a strong influence, and all the diverse Zionist movements were active there. Many Latvian Jews emigrated to Palestine.

As elsewhere, communism had great appeal for Jewish youth. To some in the younger generation, Marxism's vision of a classless society and the elimination of ethnic conflicts offered an alternative to Zionism and a beguiling solution to the "Jewish problem" in Eastern Europe. Marxist ideology was less popular with those old enough to remember the excesses committed during the Bolshevik Revolution, particularly the activities of the Yevsektsia (the Jewish department of the Cheka, the Soviet secret police, a predecessor of the NKVD and the KGB). Soviet propaganda to the contrary, most of Riga's Jews recognized Stalin as a ruthless tyrant.

The Latvian Jewish community was also divided along linguistic lines. The vast majority of Latvian Jews spoke Yiddish, but there were sizable German- and Russian-speaking enclaves. The Yiddish-speaking group included both the Orthodox and the socialists. The German speakers were the descendants of people from Courland, whereas most of the Russian-speaking group came from the province of Latgale, whose largest city was Dvinsk, as well as from other provinces of Russia. Although many Jews were fluent in Latvian, few spoke it at home or considered it their mother tongue. The German and Russian speakers represented the more assimilationist circles, and they usually had some acquaintances among and friendships with the corresponding non-Jewish population. The lack of Jews speaking Latvian was reflected in a scarcity of social contacts and friendships between Jews and ethnic Latvians. The absence of close social ties undoubtedly contributed to the almost complete lack of concern and support for Jews by the general population during the nazi years.

Riga had a number of Jewish schools offering instruction in Yiddish, Hebrew, German, or Russian. Many of these schools were associated with the different political or religious movements. After the Ulmanis' fascist putsch in 1934, the Agudat Israel, representing Habad Hasidism (Lubavitch), gained considerable influence in official circles. Working through the Ministry of Education, the group pursued an anti-Zionist policy, forcing Hebrew schools to remove Zionist content from their curricula. For example, the works and views of the poet Bialik or the famous historian Simon Dubnov were no longer politically acceptable, and it was forbidden to teach them.[6] The efforts of the orthodox notwithstanding, most Jewish intellectuals and professionals subscribed to the concept of an autonomous, secular Jewish culture.

There were many synagogues in Riga, ranging from large, beautiful edifices to small prayer houses. The largest was the Gogol Street Choral synagogue, a magnificent structure built in 1871. It was strictly orthodox with separate seating for men and women. Both Hasidim and Mitnagdim (the orthodox rabbinic opponents of Hasidism) were represented. Although the former were the more vocal, the latter were in the majority, and all the larger synagogues were controlled by the Mitnagdim. Anatol Lieven described the tensions within the Jewish community:

> By the twentieth century, hostility between Hasidim and Orthodox [i.e., Mitnagdim] had diminished in the face of the common threat of secularism and assimilation. A new three-way cultural-political struggle developed between Zionists aiming at departure for Israel and other forces, most notably the famous Bund (a Jewish Socialist Labour group . . .), which aimed at securing rights and culture of the Jews throughout the East European states.
>
> The conflict sometimes led to violence, particularly after the rise in the 1920s and 1930s of Vladimir Jabotinsky's extreme Zionist Revisionist movement, with its paramilitary wing. The particular bitterness of the dispute resulted from its being also a cultural and linguistic struggle, the Zionists promoting a secular Hebrew education while the Bund supported Yiddish, the language actually spoken at home by more than

ninety percent of the region's Jews. Conservatives and Hasidim also favoured a Hebrew educational system, but of a religious kind. All groups cut across each other, of course, to some extent.[7]

The interaction of the different religious, cultural, and political currents represented in the Jewish community of Riga stimulated a vibrant intellectual atmosphere. After the Soviet takeover, the operation of Jewish organizations in Russia was largely proscribed, and much of the Russian-oriented Jewish activity relocated to Riga. On the eve of World War II, Riga was an important center of Jewish life in Eastern Europe.

4
My Father

My father, along with his brothers, attended the Riga Stadt-Realschule, a German-language public city high school for boys. The Realschule taught modern languages—Russian, German, and French—but Latvian was not offered. The Gymnasium, the other high school in Riga, was oriented toward a classical education. In addition to Russian and German, it emphasized Latin and Greek. After completing high school, my father entered the Riga Polytechnic Institute (later Riga University), where he studied commerce (business management). He graduated with a degree in economics in 1900 and joined his father's business.

In 1888 my grandfather Max had started a factory in Riga, producing writing slates and plywood chair seats. The writing slates were supplied to elementary schools throughout Russia. After Max's younger half-brother Samuel completed his studies at the Riga Polytechnic Institute in 1899, he joined the business as manager of the plywood division. As the factory grew and prospered, Max became a merchant of the Second Guild. Around 1900, Max purchased a large parcel of land on the block between Weidendamm and Rūpniecības iela (street). Included in the purchase were several factory buildings and a large villa. The villa, at Weidendamm 35, became the family's living quarters and initially also housed the office for the adjacent factory.

After my grandfather Max's untimely death in 1908, my father took over management of the factory and greatly expanded it. Following World War I, trade between the now independent Latvia and the Soviet Union was not resumed, and the slate business collapsed. Plywood production was growing rapidly, however, and the volume of exports to Germany and England rose tremendously. Working together, my father and Uncle Eduard modernized the production facilities with new machinery imported from the West. At its peak during the mid-1930s, the

Birch logs awaiting processing in our factory yard, ca. 1932.

D. M. Michelson Furnira Fabrika (plywood factory) employed around 100 workers.

The factory was the joint property of Emma and her five children, but only my father and Eduard were actively involved in its operation. They both had a strong emotional investment in the business, which provided an income for the family in Riga and was also the primary source of support for Leo (an artist) and Clara (a writer). My grandmother felt their share of the inheritance entitled them to continuous financial support, and funds were regularly transmitted to them. In the 1920s the world's financial situation was difficult, and the business had frequent cash-flow problems. Nonetheless, Emma, my father, and Uncle Eduard offered money to Clara and Leo and regularly sent money to them in Germany and France.

My father and Uncle Eduard had occasional arguments about how to run the factory. I believe my father had ambitious ideas and was pushing for a rapid expansion of the business. Eduard seemed more conservative and possibly more realistic. The arguments usually ended inconclusively, with my father grumbling about "inhibitions."

Although my father was in charge of the factory, Emma took great interest in it and appeared to stay well informed about the state of the business. When our longtime business representative in Germany, Robert Modersohn from Bremen, made his biannual visits to Riga, Emma invariably invited him to dinner at our house. It was always a festive occasion. A heavy man in his early sixties with a florid, red-veined face, Modersohn delighted in the rich local cuisine. It became a game for Emma to urge second and third helpings on Herr Modersohn, who protested loudly but usually let himself be persuaded. The meal always ended with cream puffs, and Modersohn would consume three of these large, whipped cream–filled pastries.

Having met Modersohn on many occasions, I knew him well. During the war years we never heard from him. Realistically, he could have been of no help to us; nonetheless, I felt abandoned. In 1946 I managed to contact him in Germany. Even though I spent several weeks in Bremerhaven, we never met. As Bremen was totally destroyed, he had moved to a small town some distance away and was not able to come to the city. Later, writing to me in New York, he voiced his sincere sorrow about the terrible events. He recalled my parents and in their memory wished me and my new wife the very best. I thanked him but did not continue our correspondence.

My father was a prominent businessman and an active participant in the Jewish community of Riga, both in business circles and community affairs. He was a director of the Nordische Bank, organized by Jewish business-men, and a longtime member and chairman of the board of directors of Bikur Cholim, the local Jewish hospital. Evenings he often attended board of directors and committee meetings of his many communal involvements, and many evenings I would not see him at all. He was interested in business law and occasionally told me he wished he had studied law. A hard worker who spent long hours at the factory and many evenings doing additional preparation and planning, he always joined us for dinner, the main meal of the day, at 3:30 P.M. After an hour-long nap, he would go back to the factory, where he worked until 6:30 or 7:00.

Papa was known to procrastinate. His mother Emma, in her corre-spondence to Clara and Leo, repeatedly complained about his tendency to put things off. Even in the all-important matter of emigration, my father delayed making a decision until his freedom to act was overtaken by events. The start of World War II in 1939 and the Soviet takeover of Latvia in 1940 ended any possibility of getting out of Riga.

Papa was for me an authority figure, but I felt loved and was not afraid of him. When I was small, he called me *Häschen* (German for "little rab-bit"). I vaguely remember being spanked once when I was five or six, for some forgotten transgression. Papa was musical and had a pleasant bari-tone voice. On weekends when I was little, I sometimes listened to him sing German lieder and operatic arias while he accompanied himself on the piano. His repertoire included Schubert's "Der Lindenbaum" and arias of Leoncavallo and Wagner. I vividly recall his dramatic recital of Lohengrin's aria from Act III of the opera, when Lohengrin discloses

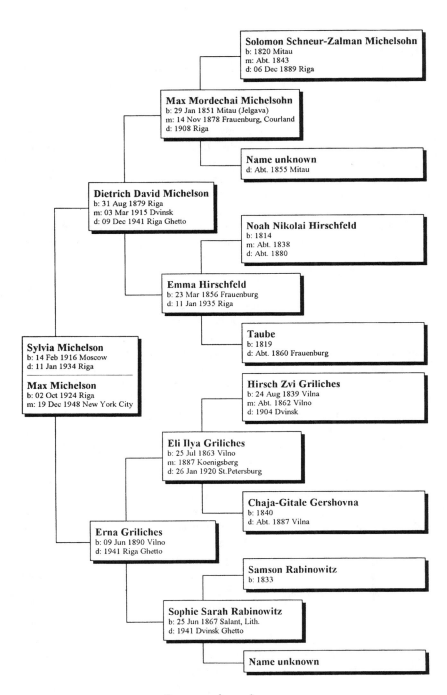

Parents and grandparents.

his identity. By the early 1930s he sang less frequently and eventually stopped altogether.

Papa had a mild case of diabetes, which he kept under control by observing a diet low in sugar and carbohydrates. Although he generally ate the same meals as the rest of the family, my mother would make sure some special foods were available for him. She bought a special cracked wheat bread, which was reserved for him alone. Every year or two, as was customary in our family, my father took the cure at a Central or Western European spa. A cure was the standard remedy for almost any ailment, and my grandmother and the five siblings constantly reminded each other that they were in need of a rest and should go take one. Customarily, they would take their cures alone. My father preferred Vichy, France, but occasionally went to Karlsbad (Karlovy Vary) in Czechoslovakia. In Vichy he always stayed at the same small pension (guest house), where he came to know the proprietor. My mother never accompanied my father on any of these trips, nor did she ever take one herself.

Our family belonged to the Peitau (Peitavas Street) Synagogue, built in 1903 and named after the street where it was located in the old-town section of Riga. During construction the congregation had experienced financial difficulties and was unable to complete the purchase of the land for the synagogue. Three Riga merchants, the president of the congregation and two board members—one of them my grandfather Max—stepped in and bought the land, thereby permitting completion of the project. After Max's death in 1908, the two remaining owners and my father (as Max's heir) deeded the land to the congregation, which unanimously voted to accept the gift at a congregational meeting in February 1909.[8] The synagogue members had permanently assigned seats. My grandfather had held a prestigious place in the sanctuary in the first row along the eastern wall—the Mizrach, a place of honor and social prominence. This seat had been retained by my father.

Papa went to services only on the High Holidays, Rosh Hashanah, and Yom Kippur and occasionally on Pesach. Our synagogue, like all places of Jewish worship in Riga, was strictly orthodox, and men and women were seated in separate sections. My mother was not religious, was not interested in observance, and, I believe, participated in the family rituals only out of respect for Father. Services at our synagogue were impressive. We had a well-known cantor, assisted by a men and boys' choir (women did not take part in the service but sat out of view on a balcony). Papa was habitually late. One Yom Kippur eve we were, as usual, tardy in arriving at services. He asked his neighbor when Kol Nidrei would be chanted, only to be told we had missed it.

In 1939 I was in a rebellious and antireligious frame of mind. That fall I refused to join Papa at the High Holiday services. He was obviously hurt but did not say anything. I regretted my behavior afterward but never talked to Papa about it. After his death I felt especially guilty about my refusal.

During my teenage years Papa and I began to spend increasingly more time together. We often took long Sunday morning walks or short off-season excursions to Jurmala, the Riga beach. One Sunday, walking near the Riga harbor, we saw a ship about to leave for an excursion, and on impulse we took the ride. It turned out to be a daylong cruise, with drinking and dancing as the main entertainment. We joined in neither and got home very late, exhausted, hungry, and bored.

In the late 1930s we frequently discussed leaving Latvia during our walks. The issue weighed heavily on my father's mind. From his perspective in Western Europe, Uncle Leo had a better sense of the impending danger. He repeatedly urged his brothers to leave Latvia. In a letter written before the German attack on the Soviet Union, Leo expressed regrets that they had not taken his advice and left the country while that was still possible. Apparently, neither my father nor Uncle Eduard believed the nazi regime posed a serious threat to us in Latvia. They tended to discount Hitler as a lunatic and could not conceive that his anti-Semitic ranting would become the official policy of the government of Germany, a civilized nation.

Papa talked about going to Palestine and also mentioned other countries but evidently did not consider any of them serious possibilities. Even then, he was no longer a young man. He knew the plywood business and preferred to remain in it. Palestine was clearly not the place for such a business. He talked about emigrating to Canada and starting a plywood business there. Canada's northern location and climate resembled that of the Baltic states, an environment my father felt was suitable for the production of plywood. Still, he had doubts about whether such a venture was feasible. He thought of himself as too old to start anew in a strange country, and he did not pursue the idea seriously. Emigration would have meant abandoning all of our property in Riga, as well as the emotional and financial investment in the factory, a step neither Papa nor Uncle Eduard was apparently able to take.

The factory was nationalized in July 1940, immediately upon the annexation of Latvia by the Soviet Union. Thea's son, my cousin Manfred Peter, was in Riga at the time and described the events in a letter to his father, Arthur, in Birmingham:

> Commissars were instituted everywhere. Ours [at the factory] was
> Gordin, our engineer. . . . Nationalization proceeded apace. Our factory
> was naturally nationalized. Indeed Gordin nationalized everything he
> could lay his hands on: properties, land, factory, machines, house & car.
> About house & car a protest was entered. I don't know what happened
> about the house, but the question about the car was settled very simply

by it being requisitioned. Last time I saw it was a few days before I left [Riga] in the courtyard of the prefecture.

My father was removed from managing the factory, and he eventually found work as an economist in another ministry. The protest about nationalization of our house was denied, and in late November 1940 we left our home and moved to a small two-bedroom apartment in Mežaparks (Kaiserwald), an upper-class residential suburb of Riga. After World War II the villa served as a dormitory for workers at our former factory. The villa was torn down in 1965 to make room for a commercial cleaning establishment. With the exception of the villa, the other buildings of the factory still stand, and the immediate neighborhood has remained unchanged to this day.

After the collapse of the Soviet Union, Latvia regained its independence in 1991, and the new government denationalized the properties taken over by the state in 1940. I was able to assert my inheritance rights and, in an ironic twist of fate, have regained possession of our family properties for my sons. The factory, which now produces quality furniture, has also been privatized. We have become majority shareholders of the new corporation. It is not a prosperous enterprise, but there is some satisfaction over having recovered it after more than fifty years.

5

My Mother and Our Home

Mama never told me how she and my father met. I believe they must have been formally introduced by a marriage broker. A contemporary photograph reveals that Mama was a beautiful woman. Having met her, Papa acted promptly and forcefully. Emma wrote to her daughter Clara that my father's sudden decision to get married caused some consternation among the mothers of Riga's eligible young women. Nevertheless, in June 1914 my father and his mother traveled to Dvinsk to meet the prospective in-laws, for the formal announcement, and to settle the dowry. In a letter to Clara, Emma described them as "very respectable and nice people, the mother-in-law is especially pleasant and *very German* [my emphasis]. The bride is pretty, but makes the impression of a good, lovely girl. For the engagement Dietrich presented her with a fine diamond ring. The wedding is planned for October, but Mr. Gr [Eli Griliches] must first deposit the money."

It was a promising match between the offspring of two well-to-do families, and Emma seems to have been impressed. The wedding had to be postponed several times because the start of World War I interfered with the preparations. There was a story relating how Erna went shopping in Germany with her mother, where they were caught by the start of the war and were able to return to Dvinsk only with great difficulty. The wedding took place at last in March 1915 and must have been an elegant affair. A copy of the menu, printed in French, lists a ten-course meal.

The war did not permit the outfitting of an apartment, and the newly-weds rented a furnished place in Riga. Within several months of their wedding, the whole Michelson family (except Clara and Leo, who were in the West) left Riga before the Germans occupied the city and moved to Moscow. When they returned to Riga in early 1919, after the war and the Russian Revolution, my parents rented an apartment in town. Several months later Emma and her younger daughter Thea went to Berlin, where they stayed for several years. Upon Emma's return in late 1921, the entire family moved back into the villa next to the factory. My mother now went to live in her mother-in-law's house. Even after my grandmother's death in the spring of 1935, my mother was not greatly concerned with or interested in running the household. Other than discussing the daily menu, she left control of the kitchen up to our cook. When we were young my sister and I had nannies, and Mama was only minimally involved in our day-to-day nurturing and supervision.

Our residence, a two-story Victorian villa designed for formal entertaining, had been built in the late nineteenth century. Down-stairs it had large rooms with high ceilings and large crystal chandeliers. There were two sitting rooms and a small library, all furnished with elegant, overstuffed sofas and chairs. The doorways were hung with dark, heavy, plush draperies. The visitor was left with a distinct impression of quiet, dignified opulence, an impression Emma had worked hard to achieve.

My mother with Sylvia, Moscow, 1916.

Although large and impressive, the villa was not a comfortable home. It was poorly insulated and drafty. There was no central heating, and the large wood-burning brick ovens did not provide an adequate and long-lasting source of heat. In the winter it was nearly impossible to maintain a comfortable temperature. During exceptionally cold weather we would get up in the morning to find the water pipes in the kitchen had frozen. More than once I overheard Uncle Eduard say to my father: "The house is uninhabitable. We must rent a modern apartment in the city." We never did. Whether it was because of the convenience of being right next to the factory or simply inertia, we continued to live there.

We were not a demonstrative family, and much passed unspoken. Nevertheless, it was not hard to see that my parents had a good marriage. They loved and respected each other. They also worked well together, my mother acting not only as office manager of our factory but also as her husband's

Our family home in Riga as drawn by Leo, 1935. I am on the right with one of my chickens.

secretary. Even though she did not use the touch-type method, she was a fast and accurate typist. My parents had occasional arguments, which could get rather loud, but they quickly blew over.

My mother grew up in Dvinsk where she had finished a Russian girls' gymnasium (high school). This was uncommon for girls of her background, who would normally not continue their formal education beyond the elementary school level. She was proud of her schooling and often talked about it. She was well read, and in addition to her first language, Russian, she was fluent in German and French. Mama was a fun-loving woman, and she particularly enjoyed the annual New Year's Ball at the Riga Jewish Club. Stylishly dressed, she went off with Papa, and they did not return until early the next morning. They would bring back fancy paper hats and other party favors, which made me feel that I, too, had been at the party.

Mama loved the movies, but my father was usually too busy to go; he thought they were a frivolous waste of time. Very occasionally my mother would persuade him to see what she considered a particularly good one. One such movie was Marlene Dietrich's *The Blue Angel,* which impressed her greatly. Although many of their friends played cards—bridge or gin rummy—my parents considered it an unseemly pastime, and they tended to look down on people who played. My mother had a number of women friends but was particularly close to Frau Hochman, a widowed dentist.

In August 1935, while spending the summer at Jurmala, my mother and I rented bicycles and went riding along the seashore. My mother had not bicycled since her childhood and was in high spirits at the prospect of again enjoying the sport. Unfortunately, shortly after we set out her bike got stuck in deep sand, and she fell and broke her ankle. She was laid up for many weeks, first in the hospital and later at home. She told me the famous Riga surgeon, Professor Vladimir Mintz, had come into her room after setting her ankle and told her she was now "like a teacup with a broken handle." She pondered this enigmatic statement at length and, not being able to make any sense of it, finally burst out crying.

After the factory was nationalized in 1940, my mother no longer went to the office. When we moved to the apartment in Mežaparks we had no servants, and Mama now ran the household and did all the cooking. I liked her cooking and thought she was a good cook.

I felt very close to Mama. She would share confidences with me and occasionally tell me jokes and anecdotes. One of her favorite stories was about a young couple on their honeymoon who had hired a carriage to take them for a ride through a park. As they were riding, the horse had some rather loud bowel movements. The embarrassed bridegroom apologized to his new bride for these "unfortunate sounds," whereupon she replied, "But I thought they came from the horse!"

On one occasion when I was about six, Mama and I were standing at my bedroom window, which overlooked our backyard. Suddenly we saw my father coming from the factory into the yard and stepping behind the corner of the large shed to urinate. (In Latvia it was acceptable to urinate outdoors.) We were amused by the sight. Nothing was said, but I felt a moment of shared intimacy with my mother.

When I was sixteen my mother and I got into a heated argument— over what has long since slipped my mind. I told her, "You are *meshuge* [crazy]." I used the Yiddish term *meshuge,* which has less weighty implications than the equivalent German *verrückt.* Still, Mama was outraged. She slapped me hard and screamed, "Don't you ever call me that again." I knew I deserved it. The incident was finished, and I felt relieved. I recall it very clearly because it was the only time Mama ever hit me.

Until I was five I had a live-in nursemaid, a middle-aged ethnic German whom we called Frau Marie. I shared a bedroom with her, and during Christmas she had a small tree in a corner of our room. She often took me to one of the city parks in our neighborhood, where I played and enjoyed watching the swans in the pond. I have little memory of her beyond that, except for a hazy recollection of having once visited St. Peters, the big Lutheran church in the Old City of Riga.

However innocuous it might seem, I suspect this visit may explain Frau Marie's abrupt dismissal. Jews did not set foot in any church. Taking a Jewish child into a church was something one did not do. Abductions of Jewish children by Orthodox clergy and forced baptisms had left a deep imprint on the Jewish psyche. For Frau Marie to have taken me there would have been considered grounds for dismissal.

My grandmother reported to Clara that "for her [Frau Marie] the parting was very sour. Bubichen [my nickname] took the separation in his stride." Her next letter indicates that Frau Marie found a new situation, but unfortunately her employers lived in a fifth-floor apartment. Frau Marie "finds taking the baby daily down and up the four flights exhausting . . . [and] is very sorry she had to leave." My mother also wrote to Clara but offered no more than that she had "let Frau Marie go" (dismissed her). She added that after Frau Marie left, I insisted that Mama stay home and take care of me. I have no memory of these demands, nor do I remember having any contact with Frau Marie after she left us.

I had two more nursemaids, both young women, in the two years following the dismissal of Frau Marie. The first was summarily discharged when she took me on an outing at which she had arranged to meet her boyfriend. I considered the outing a great adventure, but my mother took a dimmer view.

After I started school I had no more nursemaids. I spent much of my free time in the sizable yard of our factory, located right behind our house. I loved to watch the workers at their tasks, and I often invited friends to join me in my games. We used to clamber over and hide behind the high stacks of finished plywood in the warehouse of our factory. In the yard huge piles of heavy birch logs, waiting to be processed, were an irresistible attraction. My friends enjoyed visiting me and loved to roam freely in the large yard.

Uncle Eduard repeatedly voiced disapproval of my playing in the factory. He felt the piles of logs and lumber were unstable and that the yard was not a safe place to play. No doubt he was right. In my childish optimism I thought I was being careful. I was confident I could foresee and avoid any accidents. It was an exciting place for imaginative games and too inviting an opportunity to pass up. As Papa did not explicitly prohibit me from being there, I generally ignored Uncle Eduard's admonitions, although I tried to play in areas where Uncle Eduard would not see us. Even though I attempted to avoid him outdoors, I don't believe our relationship at home suffered as a result.

I was very fond of our cook Anna or, as I called her with the Latvian diminutive, Anninya. She seemed to like me, too. During the afternoon

Our cook Anninya in her kitchen, ca. 1937.

and early evening hours I often spent time with her. We talked in Latvian, and soon I became conversant, although not completely fluent, in it. I liked to watch her cook and would often help her do the dishes or other chores. Anna's bedroom was a private retreat for me. Many of my evenings were spent there comfortably ensconced in her dilapidated armchair, reading her Latvian *True Romance* magazines. As I entered my teens my Latvian improved considerably. Anna would tell an occasional off-color or raunchy anecdote, and our banter took on a more flirtatious note. My mother mildly disapproved of my spending so much time in Anna's room and occasionally told me not to bother her. But she never forbade me to go there. As long as Anna's door was open, I knew I was welcome.

Sunday was Anna's day off. She would go out or have visitors in her room. Her son and her elderly aunt came regularly. I knew Anna's visitors only by sight; she never introduced me to any of them. In fact, they appeared like a passing shadow, furtively turning the corner from the back entrance hall into the kitchen and then quickly disappearing into Anna's room. I had the impression that her visitors did not feel comfortable in our house, as if they were not sure they belonged there. Sometimes Anna also entertained boyfriends. In 1937 Anna indicated that she would soon be getting married and therefore expected to leave our employ. Her plans did not come to fruition, and Anna remained with us until we were forced to move in late 1940.

Anna and I shared a small vegetable patch in our yard and tended a few chickens. As I grew older and more ambitious, we expanded the garden. We grew tomatoes, cucumbers, radishes, and potatoes. During the summer months, when I was at the beach, Anna tended the garden by herself. I thought of the chickens as my private pets and refused to eat them. They all had names, and I recognized their individual personalities. Some of my favorites followed me through the garden and would snatch worms as I turned over the rocks that edged the walks.

In 1934 the family hired a practical nurse, Paulina Streipa, to care for my ailing grandmother. We called her *Schwester,* a term used for "nurse" in German. Her duties included keeping an eye on me. After my grandmother's death she stayed on as our housekeeper. Paulina was a widow in her forties, a tall, gaunt woman with a thin face, straight graying hair, and a sallow complexion. She did not wear lipstick, and her thin lips gave her mouth a hard, set expression. Her late husband had been a land surveyor, and she considered her present position beneath her. Installed at the head of the stairs in a windowless alcove with a low, steeply slanting ceiling, her accommodations in our house did not bespeak respect for her or for her role in the household. Her corner did not have electric lights, and its only privacy was supplied by a large movable screen.

Paulina spoke good German as well as Russian. When we were alone, she and I spoke mostly Latvian. Paulina was not a warm person; she had a disagreeable manner and what seemed like puritanical attitudes. I did not like her and occasionally made that obvious by being discourteous or even rude to her. I took my cue from Anna, who viewed Paulina as an interloper and felt she was putting on airs. Actually, Paulina did not interfere with me. By the time I was about twelve years old I was pretty much on my own, free to come and go as I pleased.

One day, while playing exuberantly in the newly fallen snow, I threw a snowball at one of the workers in the factory yard. He was a friendly fellow, and I considered it a game. Paulina, however, reprimanded me sternly: "The worker will be angry and give you a good thrashing. Your father will not be able to protect you." I knew Paulina was right; still, her rebuke annoyed me.

We took all our meals in the dining room. The room was rather dark, even during the day, because its two large windows and glass door opened onto an enclosed veranda rather than directly outside. An electric lamp, hanging low over the large dining table, was lit all the time but gave adequate lighting only immediately over the table. The rest of the room was in permanent shadow. Against the wall opposite the windows was an enormous hand-carved oak buffet that towered over the table and dominated the room. In it were kept silverware, our best dishes and tea sets, and napkins. An overstuffed couch, upholstered with a dark brown plush material, completed the furnishings but did not relieve the prevailing darkness.

Our meals were dignified occasions. The table was always set with a white tablecloth. We each had our own cloth napkin in a napkin ring alongside our place setting. After the meal we folded our napkins neatly and replaced them in the napkin rings, which had our initials or some other identifying marks. The napkins were changed weekly. We each had our regular place at the table. My father sat at the head of the table, flanked by my mother on his right and Emma on his left. Uncle Eduard sat next to my grandmother. Next to my mother sat Sylvia and then myself. Paulina Streipa also ate with us at the table, but our cook, Anna, took her meals in the kitchen. A buzzer signaled Anna when we were ready for the next course. Anna brought the food in, and my grandmother served everybody. After my grandmother's death my mother took over this duty, but our seating order did not change, and Emma's place at the table remained unfilled.

The big meal of the day was our late afternoon dinner. It consisted of three courses: soup, a main entree with potatoes and vegetables, followed by dessert. The main course invariably included a meat dish. Salads were served only during the summer months. During the winter the choice of vegetables was extremely limited—typically only carrots, cabbage (as sauerkraut), or rutabaga. The meal was accompanied by coarse black bread, but butter was never served during dinner. I believe this was a carryover from observing *kashruth,* when the main meal was fleishig (a meat meal at which dairy products could not be served). The dessert was always the same—a cranberry-based jellied compote thickened with potato starch. Called by the Russian name *kissel,* it had a beautiful dark-red color. An occasional orange or grapefruit was a luxury and a special treat. One or at most two pieces of fruit served the entire family.

Supper was a light meal served at about 7:30 P.M. It consisted of a single course: a grain, rice, or cereal dish or pasta. Fish was sometimes served, but meat dishes were never on the menu. Bread was considered essential as a precaution against choking on a fish bone. Black bread was very suitable for this purpose.

For breakfast a special brand of malt coffee was served. Even as a child I was always given malt coffee with lots of hot milk. It was an ersatz coffee, but that did not carry the pejorative implication later associated with such products. Real coffee was a delicacy reserved for afternoon teas with important visitors. Breakfast often included soft-boiled or fried eggs, generally only one to a person, and hot oatmeal porridge was sometimes served. There was a firmly held opinion that although eggs were healthful, they were to be consumed only in moderation. Eating more than one egg a day was not deemed advisable. I no longer follow these proscriptions, but I think the admonition about moderation in general, and eggs in particular, is good advice.

In elementary school we had hot lunches. Farina, occasionally lumpy, with a red cranberry-like sauce, was a staple item on the menu. In my high school hot lunches were not available, so we had to bring sandwiches. Sandwiches in Riga usually meant a solid slab of black bread with plenty of butter and some cheese or sometimes sour cream. A particular treat was a Jewish salami sandwich generously spread with rendered goose or chicken fat. Unless they had to be wrapped to be eaten later, open-faced sandwiches were the rule.

I started taking Hebrew lessons when I was about nine years old. My teacher, Herr Birnbaum, came to the house once a week. At the beginning I studied only Hebrew, but a few years later he started to prepare me for my Bar Mitzvah. I studied modern Hebrew, using the Sephardic pronunciation strongly favored by the Zionists and which was also taught in my high school. For my Bar Mitzvah, participation in the orthodox religious service required the use of the Ashkenazic or Eastern European pronunciation. The relatively minor differences in pronunciation had great religious and political implications. The Zionists had revived Hebrew as a living language, whereas for the orthodox it was a "Holy Language" not to be profaned by daily use. I considered the use of Ashkenazic in our synagogue anachronistic and resented having to use it at my Bar Mitzvah. I felt it was a gratuitous, anti-Zionist gesture, arbitrarily forced on us by the Orthodox religious establishment, and this attitude has stayed with me. Upon arriving in the United States I was surprised to discover that many synagogues still used Ashkenazic Hebrew. When I am called to the Torah, even in an orthodox synagogue, I recite the blessings using the Sephardic pronunciation.

Herr Birnbaum was an ardent Zionist. On one occasion he proudly presented me with a beautiful, small, triangular blue-and-white flag embroidered with a gold Magen David (Star of David). He spoke eloquently about Theodor Herzl and his dream of establishing a Jewish state. I liked Birnbaum, but I was not a diligent student; considering my many years of private lessons I learned relatively little Hebrew.

I was Bar Mitzvah in October 1937. For the occasion my mother outfitted me in a dark-blue suit with my first long pants. For Shabbat morning services my father, mother, and I went to the Peitau Synagogue, where I was called to the Torah. I chanted the last section of the weekly Torah portion and then the Haftarah, the prophetic portion that concludes the Torah reading on the Shabbat. I don't recall having a party for my friends, but my classmate Max Gutkin tells me he remembers attending an afternoon party at my house.

In the evening my parents hosted a large dinner party in our house for about seventy relatives and friends. Everyone was seated around a large U-shaped table. After the meal I gave two speeches, in Hebrew and in German. I had memorized the speeches written for me by Herr Birnbaum but do not recall a word I said. Everyone remarked that I had done very well. Neither Leo nor Clara could attend. Clara felt she had to stay with the ailing Thea.

My favorite present came from my parents—a bicycle. It was my first, and I used it frequently, both in the city and at Jurmala. The bike made me feel independent. I took very good care of it and cleaned it meticulously.

Uncle Eduard's gift—the modern radio receiver—enabled me to listen to stations from Western Europe and gave me a feeling of closeness, of no longer being distant from those countries. I also received many books by German Jewish authors, mostly on Jewish and Zionist themes. I found some of them difficult, but over the next few years I did finish quite a few of them.

When I was thirteen I started to see my first girlfriend. Her name was Thea. We went to the same elementary school, where Thea was one grade below me. I used to walk her home after school, but I did not tell anyone where I was going. Thea's mother worked in a library, and Thea read a lot. We spent many pleasant hours discussing books we had both read. Occasionally, however, our discussions were cut short by my abrupt exit, because I was too embarrassed to ask to use the toilet.

At home I was reluctant to disclose my true destination or to say where I had been. I would leave word that I was going to see another friend but neglected to tell that friend about it. The arrangement worked fine until one day when the friend phoned me, only to be told I had gone to see him. When I returned home I was greeted by an angry and very suspicious mother. My stuttered explanation was met with the stern question, "Who is that woman?"

6
Grandmother Sophie and the Griliches Family

My maternal grandmother Sophie lived in Dvinsk (Daugavpils in Latvian), a city 150 miles southeast of Riga. Sophie visited Riga infrequently. She was observant, and as we did not keep kosher she came mostly during Passover, when we used special kosher dishes with separate sets for meat and dairy.

Grandmother Sophie was a soft-spoken and slightly built, almost frail lady. On several occasions she fell and broke her arm or wrist, so she may have suffered from osteoporosis. Although I liked her and thought of her as a warm and loving person, I never felt as close to her as I did to Oma Emma. I did not see her often, and she devoted little time to me. I visited Sophie only once, when I was about fourteen, taking the five-hour train ride to Dvinsk by myself. I was following a precedent established by my sister Sylvia, who had gone to see our grandmother in 1929 when she was almost fourteen. I spent a week with her in her small, old, but neat and comfortable cottage where she lived with her longtime elderly maid Yosefa. A very reserved and private person, Sophie did not talk much about herself or her family. She seemed to have few visitors or friends, and I don't recall visiting any other relatives there.

Sophie (Sarah) Rabinowitz was born in Salant, a village in Lithuania. When she was an infant the family moved to Königsberg in East Prussia where she attended a girls' pension, a kind of finishing school. In February 1887 Sophie's father, Samson Rabinowitz, came to Vilna to arrange a match for his daughter with Eli (or Ilya in Russian), the oldest son of the owner of a tannery, Hirsch Zvi Griliches. The following May, Sophie visited Vilna, accompanied by her brother Baruch. The introduction was a success, and Sophie and Eli were married later that year. They settled in Vilna and had five children, four boys and one girl. The two oldest, Boris and my mother, Erna, were born in Vilna.

My grandfather Eli Griliches.

The Griliches family had lived in Vilna since at least the early eighteenth century. My great-grandfather Hirsch Zvi started the tanning business there in 1887. A few years after the death of his first wife, my great-grandmother Chaya Gitale Gershovna, he moved the factory to Dvinsk in the Vitebsk *gubernya* (province). Vitebsk was part of the Pale of Settlement, and Dvinsk, like Vilna, had a sizable Jewish population. Economic conditions inside the Pale at the end of the nineteenth century were very bad. In Dvinsk as in Vilna, the situation of the Jews was particularly precarious.

In Tsarist Russia commerce was strictly regulated, and all merchants had to belong to one of three merchant guilds. Membership in the highest, the First Guild, conferred important privileges but required a capital investment of at least 50,000 rubles. This was a considerable sum of money, comparable at the turn of the century to about U.S. $25,000. Membership also required payment of an annual tax of 528 rubles. First Guild merchants were permitted to trade throughout the Russian Empire, as well as abroad. Jewish merchants were permitted to travel and reside outside the Pale of Settlement. The Second Guild required a capital investment of 20,000 rubles and permitted its members to trade throughout the Russian Empire. Members of the Third Guild were required to have a capital investment of 8,000 rubles and were permitted to trade within their local community.[9] The 1897 census lists my great-grandfather Hirsch Zvi as a merchant of the Second Guild, but soon thereafter, as the business prospered, he joined the First Guild of St. Petersburg.

When his father relocated the business to Dvinsk, my grandfather Eli also moved there with his young family. The family lived in a rented apartment with two live-in servants. Their nurse was a Latvian peasant woman, and the cook was a Jewish woman from the province of Kovno (Kaunas in Lithuanian).

It is interesting that the 1897 census lists Yiddish as the first language of my great-grandfather's and my grandfather's family. My mother told me that at her home the family spoke Russian. In fact, all of my great-grandfather Hirsch Zvi's children seem to have spoken Russian. The switch from Yiddish to Russian must have occurred in my grandfather's generation.

All three of Hirsch Zvi's sons worked in the family business. After their father's death in 1905, my grandfather Eli and his brothers Leizer and Abram ran the business together, and all three became merchants of the First Guild. Abram, the youngest son, worked as an accountant. Leizer died in Berlin in 1912 while undergoing an appendectomy. By 1915 the factory employed over 200 people and had become the largest factory in Dvinsk. During World War I, as the city was threatened by the Germans, the factory was evacuated by rail to Rybinsk, an industrial center northeast of Moscow. The Griliches family fled to St. Petersburg (then called Petrograd).[10] While in St. Petersburg, Eli collapsed and died on the street. After the revolution the factory was nationalized, and the machinery was never returned to Dvinsk. In 1922 Abram returned to Latvia and reestablished a tannery in Dvinsk, albeit on a much smaller scale.

Uncle Boris, Sophie's oldest son, was an engineer who studied at the university in St. Petersburg. After World War I he moved to Moscow and never returned to Latvia. Boris married Anna Leonovna Danziger, originally from Riga. They had no children. We were friendly with the Danziger family in Riga, and so I heard a lot about Uncle Boris and Anna, but I never met them.

My mother was Sophie and Eli's second child and their only daughter. Her Hebrew name, as recorded in the birth register of the Crown Rabbi of Dvinsk, was Esther. She never mentioned this name to me, and in the 1897 census her name was inscribed as Erna. In the 1907 record of graduates of the Dvinsk Girls' Gymnasium, however, she was again listed as Esther.

My mother's brother Efim, or Fima, was born in Dvinsk. At the outbreak of World War I Uncle Fima was studying at the University of Karlsruhe, Germany, and was trapped there for the duration of the war. After the war, having received his degree of Diplom-Engineer in Chemistry with a specialty in tanning, he worked for several years in Germany. In 1923 Fima received permission from the Latvian government to return to Dvinsk, where he worked for his Uncle Abram in the newly reestablished tannery. In 1928 an accident occurred at Abram's factory. Abram blamed Fima for it and fired him on the spot. Relations between my granduncle Abram and my grandmother Sophie became strained, and the rift also extended to their families. After the war I visited Abram's daughter Genya Balson, who now lives in Israel, but I never met my granduncle or any other members of his family. Judging from conversations between my parents, I was under the impression that Abram did not give a share of the business income or any financial support to his sister-in-law, Eli's widow, Sophie.

Uncle Fima married Clara Ziv, and soon after their marriage the newlyweds moved to Kaunas, at that time the capital of Lithuania. Fima took a position in his in-laws' cigarette factory. My mother once com-

Family gathering, Riga, 1928. Left to right: Mischa, Nyura, Grandmother Sophie, Fima, Sylvia, my mother, myself, my father, Grandmother Emma.

mented that Fima would have been happiest in an academic environment. Unfortunately, academic appointments were not open to Jews in prewar Lithuania. In sharp contrast to her more reserved husband, Clara was a beautiful and vivacious young woman. They had two children, my cousins Zvi and Ellen.

Sophie would occasionally visit Fima and his family in Kaunas, and sometimes they came to see us in Riga or at Jurmala. I met Uncle Fima several times, and my mother talked about him frequently. Fima was a charming man with a delightful sense of humor. I liked him and felt I knew him well. During our meetings Fima was attentive to me; he would always tell me an anecdote or pose a puzzle. I first met my cousin Zvi, then called Garrik, during a summer in the early 1930s when his family visited us at Jurmala. My cousin Ellen had not yet been born.

Uncle Mischa, Sophie's third son, and his wife, Nyura, lived in Paris where they ran an art gallery. They had no children. Mischa's relationship with his family was strained, although I do not know why. Sometime during the Russian Civil War, when the family was living in St. Petersburg, Mischa left home. He may have been conscripted into the Red Army but later managed to join a White Army unit in Archangelsk. The Whites were counterrevolutionary forces fighting against the Bolsheviks. When the foreign interventionist forces evacuated Archangelsk, Mischa managed to go with them and eventually found his way to Paris. There Mischa met and married Nyura, who had moved from Riga to Paris despite the strong objections of

Clara Ziv Griliches, 1935.

her father. Her parents were worried about her living in Paris alone and wanted her to meet a nice, suitable young man. They heard that Mischa was living in Paris, and introductions were made long distance. Nyura, who had misgivings, was pleasantly surprised when she met the handsome Mischa.

In 1928, shortly after their marriage, Nyura and Mischa visited Riga. We were all impressed by Nyura, a diminutive woman, very spirited and exuberant. She was *très chic*—a real Parisienne. In addition to my grandmothers and the newlyweds, Uncle Fima had joined us on this occasion. We posed in our home for a group photograph, which survived the war among Boris and Anna's possessions in Moscow. In Paris, Mischa and Nyura did maintain contact with my uncle Leo and aunt Clara, yet a certain coolness and distance remained between Mischa and the rest of the family. Mischa died in 1979. Nyura still lives in Paris and continues to run their art gallery.

Sophie's youngest boy, Alexander (known by the Russian diminutive Sascha), remained in St. Petersburg (Leningrad) after World War I. To return to Latvia required the permission of both the Soviet and Latvian governments, neither of which was anxious to grant it. Sophie did not return to Dvinsk until 1925. By that time Sascha had finished college, but being of draft age, he was not permitted to leave the Soviet Union. Sophie may have been drawn to Dvinsk by the presence there of Fima, who had already returned from Germany, and by Erna who was then back in Riga. Sascha was a chemical engineer. He did not marry and lived in Leningrad.

Although none of Sophie's children lived in Dvinsk, all except Mischa lived reasonably close. Unlike the Michelson siblings, Sophie's children seem not to have maintained close contact. At the time people ordinarily kept in touch through letters, although emergency news might be communicated by telegram. Even where telephones were available, long-distance calls were almost never made. Sophie did not even have a telephone. The siblings may have corresponded, but they seldom visited each other. Although distances among Riga, Dvinsk, and Kovno were not large, it took a five-hour train ride to get there. Erna visited her mother only every few

The brothers Griliches, Moscow, 1935. Left to right: Fima, Sascha, Anna (Boris's wife), Boris.

years. Of her four brothers, my mother seemed closest to Fima, yet I do not remember her ever going to Kovno. I have the impression that my mother was very fond of Anna, who lived with Boris in Moscow. They were especially close during the war years, when they both lived in Moscow.

Geographically, Moscow was reasonably close (as was Leningrad, where Sascha lived). Politically, however, the Soviet Union was another world. Communications with the USSR were never good, and contacts with friends and relatives there were irregular. After returning to Dvinsk, Sophie never saw Boris or Sascha again.

Although visits to the Soviet Union were possible during the 1920s, they became increasingly difficult under Stalin after the early 1930s. During the years of the Stalin terror, the Bolsheviks discouraged all communications with the West. People in the Soviet Union were afraid to write or receive letters or even to acknowledge having relatives in capitalist countries. In 1935 Uncle Fima was able to visit his two brothers in Moscow. He had not seen either of them since before World War I, more than twenty years earlier. A photo taken on this occasion recorded what they had no way of knowing would be their last reunion. On his way home to Kaunas, Fima stopped in Riga and brought us news of them. After that time we heard nothing.

Erna never knew her youngest brother, Sascha, as an adult; during

World War I, when she was in Moscow, he lived in St. Petersburg. Sascha disappeared during the purges in the late 1930s. We assumed he had been arrested by the People's Commissariat of Internal Affairs (NKVD), a fate shared by millions during Stalin's reign. Details about his fate emerged only recently, after the collapse of the Soviet Union. Sascha, who was not a member of the Communist Party, was manager of a department in a state chemical industrial complex. In 1937 he was arrested on the charge of "being an agent of German intelligence, engaged in sabotage-wrecking activities in the Ochtinsky Chemical Combinat." Convicted and sentenced to be shot, Sascha was executed in December 1937. He was thirty-four years old. In 1957, as Stalin's misdeeds were exposed after his death, Sascha was posthumously cleared and rehabilitated by the Supreme Court of the Soviet Union.

Although my mother had a number of uncles, aunts, and cousins, none of them lived in Riga. Once I met a cousin from Dvinsk, Grischa Rafalowitz, the son of my mother's aunt Rosa. Rosa was my grandfather Eli's youngest sister, just ten years older than my mother. Grischa, a deaf-mute, visited us in Riga, and we conversed in a makeshift sign language. His visit remains fresh in my mind. His younger brother Schura (now Alexander Rafaeli) studied at Riga University in the mid-1930s. He also came to see us several times, but I have no recollection of his visits. After completing his studies, Schura emigrated to Israel.

In 1941 my grandmother Sophie was forced into the Dvinsk Ghetto, where she was murdered by the nazis. My mother's aunt Rosa Rafalowitz, her husband, Boris, and son, Grischa, were also trapped in Dvinsk and killed during the liquidation of the ghetto. Sophie's brother-in-law Abram managed to hide in his factory. In September 1944, just days before Dvinsk fell to the advancing Red Army, Abram, believing the city had already been liberated, ventured forth from his hideout. He was caught and killed by the nazis.

7
Sylvia

My sister, Sylvia, was born in 1916 in Moscow. The family had moved there the previous year when Riga was threatened by the Germans. Quiet, studious, and hard-working, Sylvia was a diligent student who prided herself in getting top grades in all her subjects. When I was very young she would sometimes play with me in our yard, but once Sylvia started high school she spent most of her time at home doing schoolwork. Then she seldom played with me, and I saw little of her except at mealtimes.

Sylvia's room was off my parents' bedroom, with no connection directly from the hall. Originally, it had been the dressing room for the master bedroom, and it could be entered only by way of my parents' bedroom. Her room was smaller and darker than mine. (I may have been given the larger room because I shared it with my nurse.) In the evening her desk lamp cast a small circle of light just on her work, leaving the rest of the room in almost total darkness. Sylvia always seemed to be writing. She usually rewrote her copious notes and composed what seemed to me overlong essays. I was amazed and baffled by her disciplined work habits and, in particular, by her powers of concentration. It never occurred to me to interrupt her or to ask her to play with me.

Sylvia attended Luther School, a private German-language elementary and high school for girls. It was a school for children of the Baltic German "aristocracy" and had a reputation for not accepting Jews into the high school. Nonetheless, both Sylvia and two of her girlfriends were admitted.

I don't believe Sylvia was friendly with any of her non-Jewish classmates, but she did have a few close girlfriends. Her best friend was her classmate Irma Danziger, the niece of my mother's sister-in-law Anna Danziger Griliches. Sylvia did not go out much, and I do not remember that she ever dated.

Thea and Sylvia, Moscow, 1917.

Sylvia entered Riga University in the fall of 1933. A few months later she developed a middle-ear infection that turned into meningitis. As her condition worsened, my father sent for a specialist, a famous professor from Vienna. He arrived too late to be of help. Sylvia died just short of her eighteenth birthday. Seven years later penicillin first became available. Her death, a terrible blow for us all, was particularly devastating for my mother. My mother and Sylvia were extremely close, and Sylvia had been the joy of Mama's life. Mama would recall what an adorable baby Sylvia had been and how she and Nyanya, her Russian nanny, had proudly paraded through Moscow wearing a little fur coat. People would stop to admire the beautiful chubby little girl. With Sylvia's death my mother became profoundly depressed. She never entirely recovered from this loss.

A recollection: Coming home on an early winter afternoon, I find Mama standing in our dining room surrounded by several women friends. Outside, dusk is beginning to settle, and the room is dark. As the women step aside to make room for me, I run up to Mama and embrace her. "Mami, Mami, I am here for you," I say. Crying, she kisses me and turns back to her friends. Feeling left out and disappointed that my attempt at consoling Mama has failed, I retreat to my room.

The somber mood in our house was aggravated by a collusion among the family to keep the death secret from my grandmother Emma, who was gravely ill at the time. Emma suffered from congestive heart failure, and the family feared she would not survive the bad news. Accordingly, on doctor's orders, Emma was confined to bed in her upstairs room even as my sister's funeral was proceeding in the big parlor downstairs. My grandmother was told Aunt Clara had taken Sylvia to a clinic in Paris for further treatment. Grandmother Sophie, who knew of Sylvia's death, did not come to Riga for the funeral. I was excluded from the family circle at this solemn occasion and was sent to spend the day with my cousin Ali Kretzer. I can only guess whether this was done to avoid arousing my grandmother's suspicions or because I was thought to be too young to understand and participate in the sad happening. Whatever the reason, I felt left out and alone.

To maintain the fiction that Sylvia was still alive, Clara went to Paris and wrote letters to her mother in Sylvia's name. This continued until my grandmother's death a year later. Clara surely concurred in the decision to keep Sylvia's death a secret, although it must have been especially painful for her not to see her mother again. In a letter to Clara dated May 1934, Eduard wrote, "I can imagine how difficult it is for you to write letters to Mama, but, unfortunately, nothing can be changed."

I considered the whole situation bizarre. I think my grandmother may well have sensed what had happened but chose to join in the denial. Maintaining this charade also precluded any overt expression of mourning. It meant that none of us, particularly my

Grandmother Emma with Sylvia, Riga, 1923.

mother, was able to grieve openly. We did little visiting and entertaining, and a pervasive sadness and emptiness settled like a pall over our home. It was not until my Bar Mitzvah, more than three years later, that a joyous occasion was again celebrated in our family.

8
My Aunts and Uncles

Of my aunts and uncles I knew my father's sisters and brothers best. Aunts Clara and Thea and Uncle Leo visited Riga nearly every year, and Uncle Eduard lived and shared his meals with us. I knew them all well and considered them members of the immediate family.

CLARA

Aunt Clara, Emma and Max's second child and oldest daughter, was a tiny woman who never married. My grandmother told me she was sure Clara's growth had been stunted because as a little girl she had a dark room. After World War II I heard that when she was young she had fallen in love with an uncle, her father's younger half-brother Eduard (not to be confused with Clara's brother, my uncle Eduard). This uncle was just nine years older than Clara. It was thought that because Clara could not marry him, she chose to remain single.

I know little about Clara's formal education. She must have finished a German high school for girls in Riga. Clara, like all the Michelson siblings, was fluent in German, Russian, and French. In the early 1900s Clara took courses in sociology and philosophy with Georg Simmel, a well-known professor at the University of Berlin. Clara also attended lectures by Sigmund Freud in Vienna. Freud's explicit emphasis on human sexuality may have been uncomfortable for her, and she found Adlerian psychology more congenial. She took courses and was thoroughly conversant with Alfred Adler's *Individual Psychology,* which she discussed with me. Clara was also interested and well versed in graphology. Her article "The Symbol in Signature" was published in *La Graphologie Scientifique* in 1936 in Paris.

The start of World War I caught Clara in Germany. She was able to return to Russia, probably by way of Stockholm, in 1916. By that time the family had already escaped Riga and gone to Moscow. In early 1917 Clara went with her mother to the Caucasus and stayed there after Emma returned to Moscow. After the start of the revolution, fighting between the Bolsheviks and Allied interventionist forces trapped Clara in the south. She managed to get to Yalta in the Crimea, where she spent almost two years. Leo was instrumental in obtaining permission for her to come to Germany. Traveling by way of Constantinople and Italy, Clara was finally able to join him in Berlin in 1920. She eventually settled in Paris and worked as a writer. Except for occasional visits, she never returned to Riga. In the early 1930s she moved to Berlin, but like her brother Leo, she was soon back in Paris. Clara supported herself with income from her share of the family business, which Dietrich and Eduard sent her regularly. She occasionally helped by making contacts with our agents in Western Europe.

On her visits to Riga, particularly while my grandmother was alive, Clara spent extended periods with us. She took great interest in me and devoted much time to playing and talking with me. She had a calm, thoughtful manner and often expressed her psychological insights in her talks with me. She always treated me like a reasonable, responsible person. Clara had an effective way of dealing with my occasional temper tantrums. She would engage me in quiet conversations aimed at exploring my frustrations and would help me find more constructive ways of understanding and expressing them. She was also interested in dream interpretation. I told her my dreams, which she recorded, and we discussed possible interpretations. I loved her dearly.

Clara wrote in both German and French, and some of her early stories were in Russian. From 1910 to 1913 she was a regular contributor to *Die Wage,* a Viennese weekly that published several of her short stories, as well as her essays "The Legacy of Tolstoy" and "Ibsen's Brand and Kant's Categorical Imperative." In 1936 in Berlin, Philo Verlag, a well-known Jewish publisher, printed a small volume of Clara's short stories in German, *Jüdisches Kind aus dem Osten* (A Jewish Child from the East), which Clara dedicated to the memory of her niece Sylvia. The book was widely reviewed in Jewish newspapers, including the *New York Forverts,* and a Yiddish translation appeared in Riga in 1937 under the title *Di Yidishe Neshome* (The Jewish Soul). Clara also prepared a French translation but was apparently unable to find a publisher.

I do not know to what extent Clara shared the family's negative feelings about Yiddish. It is clear, however, that she was eager to have her book translated and published in Yiddish. She carefully arranged for the translation and kept a scrapbook containing the reviews and editorial comments that subsequently appeared in the Yiddish press.

Although Clara was not interested in Judaism as a religion, much of her work addressed Jewish themes. It dealt with Jewish life in Eastern Europe in cultural and humanistic rather than political terms. Her chosen topics reflected her concern with psychological and sociological issues, as well as the position of women in Eastern European society. In reviewing her various writings, I conclude that Jewish life held greater importance in her thinking than I had been aware of.

In a last-minute effort to escape the 1940 onslaught of the nazis on Paris, my uncle Leo managed to hire a broken-down taxi and went to Nantes with his sisters, Clara and Thea. Leo wanted to continue on to the south of France and tried to persuade his sisters to join him. Clara, however, was adamant. She and Thea were not going any farther. They were going to go back to Paris and stay there. After all, she knew the Germans. What would Germans do to them? Frustrated, Leo caught the last train to Bordeaux and went on alone.

Back in Paris, a few months before the German attack on the Soviet Union, Clara, a Latvian national, applied to the German authorities for permission to return to Riga. The permission never came. Instead, she was eventually taken to the Sammellager (assembly camp) at Drancy. On July 27, 1942, Clara was deported to Auschwitz, where she was killed upon arrival. From her transport of 1,000 persons there were just 11 survivors, among them only 2 women.[11] Thea, a British subject, was not harmed by the nazis.

Following the war, Leo was able to retrieve Clara's remaining possessions from Paris. Among her extensive notes and many papers were a number of copies of *Di Yidishe Neshome* and completed manuscripts of two unpublished novels. I have given the surviving copies of Clara's book to the National Yiddish Book Center in Amherst, Massachusetts, and was recently gratified to learn that copies have been placed in the Yiddish collections of several university libraries. The novels are *Sünde wider den Geist* (Sin Against the Spirit), a psychological work dedicated to N. Minsky; *Wölfleins Liebe* (The Love of Little Wolf), a novel about the life of a child; and a considerable number of short stories, fairy tales, and fables in German and in French.

EDUARD

Uncle Eduard lived in the family home and took most of his meals there. Even so, he maintained an independent and private lifestyle. Uncle Eduard lived in a two-room suite with a separate entrance directly off the rear entrance of our house. He had a large, comfortably furnished living room with a centrally placed desk; a large, well-filled bookcase; and a large couch. Beyond the living room lay a small, sparsely furnished bedroom. Eduard shared bathroom facilities in the main house with the rest of us. His rooms were always locked, but a key hung in the kitchen. Still, I never felt at liberty to explore his suite, as I did the rest of the house. I loved to rummage through the attic and library and in my parents' bedroom and desk drawers, but Eduard's room was always off limits to me and was therefore a place of mystery. He had many friends and often received visitors in his apartment. Its direct entrance afforded him considerable privacy. Despite my curiosity, I was unable to observe his guests' comings and goings. Emma's repeated efforts to arrange a suitable match came to naught. Eduard never married. Apparently, it was a well-known secret that he had a long-term relationship with a married woman.

Eduard was short but solidly built. In school he had been a good athlete—a gymnast who performed on parallel bars and the horizontal bar. When I knew him during the 1930s, he was no longer athletically inclined. I have several photos of Eduard and his cousins in bathing suits at Jurmala. One weekend the sudden, infrequent exposure to the intense noontime sun resulted in a severe sunburn that kept him in bed for several days. After that, during his occasional weekend visits to our summer place he remained fully dressed, and even at Jurmala Eduard did not wear casual clothes but was always attired in suit and tie. Eduard was not unique; at that time in Riga, men's leisure wear was practically unknown.

Uncle Eduard sometimes questioned me about school, my friends, and my opinions and ideas. He wanted to know what my friends and I were interested in and what we talked about, how classes were conducted, how we behaved in class, what we thought of our teachers, and similar topics. These questions occasionally led to longer discussions, and he seemed genuinely interested in learning more about my school and the current youth culture.

Eduard, like all of Max and Emma's children, was born in Riga. After graduating from the Riga Stadt-Realschule, Eduard studied at the Riga Polytechnic Institute. Neither he nor my father told me much about their school years. Eduard was a mechanical engineer and the technical director of our factory. He was very interested in social issues and concerned with the workers' welfare. He was, I believe, well liked by them. In a letter to Clara in 1937, Eduard proudly described a Christmas party he had given for our workers and their families that was attended by around 300 people.

Eduard had been a member of the Bund, the Jewish socialist movement, and was involved in the 1905 revolution. According to Uncle Leo, Eduard had run a small printing press. After World War I and the ensuing revolution, he did not return immediately to Riga with the other family members but remained in the Soviet Union. He worked in Moscow as an engineer. Eduard visited Riga in 1919, but he had difficulty getting permission to reside in Latvia and did not return to Riga until 1923. He retained strong socialist beliefs, and in the Latvian democratic elections prior to the coup under Ulmanis in 1934, he supported the Social Democrats, as did the rest of my family. During the Spanish Civil War, our local newspapers were strongly pro-Franco. Once, when Eduard saw me reading the paper, he admonished me not to believe any of the reports about the Spanish Civil War, which were printed under pressure from the Latvian fascist government. According to Eduard, it was just propaganda, not at all the truth.

After the factory was nationalized, Eduard became its executive director and continued to work there. The local commissar placed in charge of the factory after the Soviet takeover was Gordin, an engineer who had previously worked under Eduard. In the ensuing power struggle between the two, Gordin sought the support of party officials from Moscow, whereas Eduard had the votes of our workers. Eventually, the matter was brought up for a decision to the Communist Party, which bowed to the preference of our workers and ruled in Eduard's favor.

Eduard was an intellectual. He was especially interested in psychology, and his library included many works on the topic. Freudian theories and psychoanalysis provided inexhaustible topics of conversation. "What do you think of Freud?" was his standard opener for such discussions. In the 1920s and 1930s Riga's middle-class Jewish society remained strongly influenced by Victorian standards. Freudian emphasis on sexuality, particularly the sexuality of the child, ran counter to the professed, if not the practiced, morality. Typical of this attitude was the Yiddish adage: everybody knows what the bride and the bridegroom do after the *chuppah* (literally the wedding canopy, but meaning the wedding ceremony), but he who talks about it is a boor. Some years later in the camps, my friend and mentor Mulya Atlas quoted this saying and advised me to observe it.

In our family the term *Talmudic* had negative overtones; it referred to casuistry and extreme pedantry. I do not know whether Eduard had first-hand knowledge of orthodoxy or what kind of religious training he had received. He and my father, the two oldest boys in the family, probably had a private tutor come to the house. I do not believe they ever attended a heder (religious elementary school). In contrast to my father, Eduard was strongly antireligious and was particularly outspoken in his dislike of orthodox institutions, the heder, and the yeshiva (Talmudic academy). For him Judaism was the ultra-Orthodox, repressive religion of the shtetl (small Eastern European town or village), exemplified by the crushing and stultifying atmosphere of the heder. The heder was traditionally presided over by an impoverished and embittered schoolmaster, the *melamed*. The rabbi was generally revered, but the *melamed* was scorned as an inadequate scholar who strained to earn a living by teaching recalcitrant pupils. Eduard never attended services, but he questioned me repeatedly about my religious studies and religious school. Although he joined us at family religious gatherings such as the Passover seder, he never participated in the prayers, nor did he wear a hat as was customary during religious observances in our house. On one occasion when I was about twelve, I brought Uncle Eduard's hat and handed it to him. There was silence around the table. Eduard put the hat aside, and we proceeded with the observance. My action was insolent, and my uncle must have resented it deeply. Yet at the time I did not appreciate my impertinence or know enough to apologize.

The orthodox Jewish religious establishment in Latvia alienated a large section of the nonorthodox Jewish population. In the Saims (the Latvian Parliament), Agudat Israel (the Jewish Orthodox party), under the leadership of Mordechai Dubin, generally supported the right-wing Peasant Party led by Karlis Ulmanis against the left-wing socialists and the other Jewish deputies. Ulmanis became prime minister and in 1934 engineered a coup and pronounced himself head of an authoritarian dictatorship. Under the Ulmanis regime the Agudat Israel became the official arbiters of Judaism at the Ministry of Education. Jewish schools were closed on Shabbat but open on Sundays; Jewish male teachers had to be observant, and all boys had to attend daily minyan (morning service). Dubin, although strictly observant, tried to help all Jews in difficulty and made no distinction between the observant and the nonobservant.[12]

Eduard was preoccupied with the so-called Jewish question: How should the situation of the Jews in Eastern Europe be resolved? The polarities of communism, socialism, Zionism, and the many other ideologies provided endless topics for argument and discussion. Eduard's outlook was pro-Zionist, probably labor-Zionist. In 1938 he took me along on a visit to a *hachsharah*, an agricultural training farm for would-be *chalutsim*—pioneers—to Palestine. The farm was an hour's ride from Riga. It seemed to me that Eduard was well acquainted with many of the people there and must have been a supporter of that movement. I overheard numerous discussions of the concepts and practices of the Kibbutz movement, particularly the idea of shared, communal property. The left-wing Hashomer Hatzair movement was very extreme and doctrinaire in its insistence on the elimination of all private property. Eduard's admiration of communal ideals was tempered by his doubts about these practices and his reluctance to personally commit to them.

The rising threat of National Socialism in Germany and the brutal regime in the Soviet Union (at that time we did not perceive the Soviets as overtly anti-Semitic) made the issue of Jewish survival critical. The question "Where should the Jews go?" was particularly acute. Birobidjan, the short-lived Soviet solution for a Jewish homeland, was never considered seriously. It was viewed as a curiosity, not a viable answer to the problem. Alternate solutions, such as Uganda, were often discussed and mostly rejected. In fact, however, in the late 1930s no countries accepted Jews, and Eastern European Jews had no place to go.

Like the majority of Riga's Jews, Eduard was caught there by the nazi invasion. His fate in the Riga Ghetto is described in Chapter 15.

LEO

My uncle Leo, the youngest son of my grandparents, was an artist. He started painting at an early age. His earliest work, landscapes and small portraits, showed great promise. When he was seventeen and still in high

Leo Michelson, 1938.

school, two of his works were included in an exhibition of Baltic painters at the Museum of the City of Riga. After finishing the Riga Stadt-Realschule in 1906, Leo, against his father's wishes, went to Munich where he was admitted to the Bavarian Academy of Fine Arts. His father later agreed to provide an allowance so Leo could continue his studies in Munich. In 1908 Leo applied to the Academy of Fine Arts in St. Petersburg. He passed a tough entrance competition and was admitted to the academy. But Leo found the academic atmosphere stifling and dropped out after several months of fitful attendance. He then enrolled in the Dorpat (Tartu) University medical school to study anatomy, and after completing the course, he returned to Riga.

Upstairs in one wing of our villa was an unheated attic room that had once been Leo's atelier. When I was growing up, the studio had long been abandoned and neglected. Hanging in the room was a skeleton, a leftover from Leo's anatomical studies, which gave the place an air of spookiness. Electric lights had never been installed in the studio. Although I found the studio fascinating, I never dared go there after dark.

Leo made frequent trips to Berlin and in 1910 visited Paris for the first time. While in Berlin he was introduced to Lovis Corinth; the meeting developed into a friendship that lasted until Corinth's death. Corinth used Leo as the model for the central figure of Christ in his famous *Ecco Homo*. The painting evoked some critical comment for portraying a too Semitic Jesus. In 1937, pronounced as "degenerate art" by the nazis, it was sold to a museum in Basel, Switzerland.[13]

During the years before World War I, Leo traveled extensively through Italy, France, Germany, and the Crimea. While traveling he spent many hours visiting museums in every city, and he could always recall the various works on exhibit and where he had seen them. Leo developed an encyclopedic knowledge of art and the history of painting. He had a connoisseur's eye for recognizing old masters and could correctly attribute paintings, even when the artist was obscure.

During World War I he was stranded in Germany, but in 1918 he was able to return to Riga and reclaim the family property from the German occupation authorities. After the war Leo made his home first in Berlin, then in 1932 he moved to Paris.*

In 1932 Leo was invited by Anatoly Lunacharsky, the Soviet commissar of education, to exhibit in the Soviet Union. Lunacharsky, a personal friend, made it clear to Leo that the situation in the country was deteriorating. It was several years before the start of Stalin's purge trials, but Leo had a premonition of impending catastrophe.

Leo was a charming man who radiated a vitality that made it a delight to be in his company. He would talk with great enthusiasm about various aspects of art and painting. He could also be an attentive and engaging conversationalist and would listen with interest to his acquaintances. In his travels he met many fascinating people and developed a great many lasting friendships. His charming personality masked an iron determination and persistence that became particularly evident in matters relating to his art. Like many artists, Leo was ambivalent about selling his work. On the one hand he was pleased that people wanted to buy his paintings; however, he found parting with them painful. It was as though they were his children, and one does not sell one's children. He was thrilled when he was able to regain possession of a painting he had sold, occasionally using the pretext that he wanted to make a small change or an improvement.

Many of his works remained in our family home in Riga, where they were lost during World War II. This loss pained him greatly. When we met in New York after World War II, he questioned me repeatedly as to the circumstances under which the paintings were abandoned in our house or in the suburban apartment we moved to after our house was nationalized by the Soviets. We took a few pictures with us to the apartment, and my father moved most of the others to a storage shed on the only one of our properties that had not been nationalized. After the German occupation of Riga we were forced into the Ghetto and had to leave behind all the works in the apartment. Those in the storage shed were similarly abandoned.

In 1937, in recognition of his artistic achievements, the French government awarded Leo the Cross of Chevalier of the Legion of Honor—a signal honor, especially for a foreign artist. As Leo was a Latvian national, the approval of the Latvian government was needed. Despite the fact that Leo had close friends in Latvian artistic and intellectual circles, permission was only grudgingly extended. The Latvian Academy initially tried to derail the award, claiming Michelson was an unknown. Among Leo's Latvian friends was the painter Ludolfs Liberts, then director of the state printing

---

*For an account of Leo's life and work see the monograph by Rainer Esslen, *A Joy to Paint: The Life of Leo Michelson* (Marshall, TX: Michelson Museum of Art, 1998). Color reproductions of Leo's work can be found in Jean Bouret, *Leo Michelson* (New York: Arts, Inc., 1963).

Jennie Tourel, New York, ca. 1944. Courtesy, Roman Vishniac.

office, who lobbied on Leo's behalf. When it became clear that permission to accept the award was only a formality and that Leo was going to be honored by the French, the Latvians reconsidered. The state awarded Leo the Three Star Order of Culture of The Latvian Republic, and an exhibition of Leo's work was hurriedly organized at the Riga City Museum of Art.

The exhibition opened to good reviews in January 1938, and the museum bought *The Tahitian Girl,* one of Leo's more exotic paintings. This painting remains in the museum's possession, but it is not on display. In a curious repetition of history, the current curator does not know anything about Leo Michelson the artist.

In 1937 Leo met Jennie Tourel, an operatic mezzo-soprano at the Opéra Comique in Paris. Jennie had been born Jennie Davidson to Russian parents. After World War I the family settled in Paris. She took her stage name from her singing teacher, El-Tour. In spring of 1939 Leo announced their intention to marry and brought Jennie to meet the family in Riga. During this visit she was invited to perform the title role in *Carmen* at the Riga State Opera. That performance was my introduction to opera. I was very taken by Jennie's singing and acting, and the whole experience impressed me greatly. Jennie created a minor stir by lighting a cigarette during the seduction scene and then casually tossing it away. The dramatic impact of the gesture was somewhat eclipsed by a stagehand, who quickly stepped in to extinguish the offending cigarette.

After the war Leo told me that during that visit he had asked his brothers to pay him his share of the business. He felt he needed the financial security to get married. Dietrich and Eduard put him off; they did not have liquid funds and were not in a position to give him his share at that time. Apparently, Leo did not insist. Although Jennie and Leo considered themselves married, I don't believe they actually had a marriage ceremony. It may not have been the only consideration, but the perception that his financial situation was inadequate contributed to Leo's not formalizing their union.

In 1940, when the German army was threatening Paris, Leo managed to escape to southern France with Minos, his miniature French poodle. Jennie Tourel, who had left Paris ahead of him, anxiously greeted him at the station in Bordeaux. In Toulouse Leo painted a portrait of the wife of the Portuguese consul, which helped in obtaining Portuguese visas. Once in Lisbon, Leo was able to organize an exhibition of his work and sold several of his paintings, some of which he had created on the spot. While still in Lisbon, Jennie became seriously ill with typhoid fever but eventually recovered. After a difficult and perilous journey, they arrived in New York in late 1940.

9

Thea, Arthur, and Manfred Peter

My aunt Thea was the baby in Grandmother Emma's family. She died in 1977, having retained her childlike innocence and sweetness until the end. She once told us that even as an old person she still felt like a young girl.

Thea was the only one of Emma's children whose marriage plans Emma was able to influence. The others were independent-minded and would not even consider Emma's suggestions in this important matter. As Thea became of marriageable age, Emma began looking for a suitable husband. It was important that Thea's future husband have a German background. Accordingly, after World War I Emma took Thea—a pretty, petite woman with a good dowry—to Berlin in the hope of finding a suitable match. Arthur Percy Sommerfeld met all the conditions Emma thought important: he was tall and handsome and, above all, of German Jewish background. His prospects were exceptional. Thea and Arthur were married in Berlin in 1921. Her mission accomplished, Emma returned to Riga to resume her place as the family matriarch.

Arthur was born to German Jewish parents in Melbourne, Australia. He had graduated from the Technische Hochschule (technical college) in Berlin in 1907 with the degree Diplom-Ingeneur in machine design. A specialist in the new, rapidly developing field of plastics, Arthur was the plant manager of a plastics factory in Berlin. In 1920 Arthur moved to Freiburg am Breisgau in southwest Germany, where he became the managing director of a factory that produced plastic insulators for electric power circuits. He held a number of patents, authored two books on plastics, and was recognized as an authority on injection molding.

The Sommerfelds lived in Freiburg, a beautiful area on the Rhine close to the Black Forest. Here their only child, Manfred Peter, was born. Arthur's mother, Bertha (or Mutti, as she was called), lived with them. They had a beautiful house with servants, and they lived in comfortable circumstances surrounded by a congenial community. Thea's letters from Freiburg tell of a busy social life: visits to friends and excursions and longer trips with friends. The Sommerfelds did not belong to a synagogue or observe Jewish holidays. Although they moved mostly in Jewish circles, like most of their friends they observed Christmas. Peter was not Bar Mitzvah.

My grandmother Emma visited them occasionally, but during the summer holidays Thea and Peter would regularly come to Jurmala, where they usually spent six to eight weeks. Arthur often came with them but was able to stay only a couple of weeks.

My cousin Manfred, or Peter as he was called after the family moved to England, was eighteen

Thea and Arthur, Freiburg, ca. 1926.

months my senior. We liked each other and got along well, and I viewed Peter as virtually an older brother. Peter was not only older; he lived in the technologically and culturally more advanced Western Europe and was more sophisticated and traveled than I, who had never been out of Latvia. During our summer vacations at the beach we were continually together and got to know each other. We had a wonderful time, free to come and go and roam as we pleased with little supervision and no interference from our elders. I think we both looked forward to these vacations. On rainy days we would spend hours sitting on the porch and drawing pictures. Peter was particularly adept at elaborate futuristic drawings of ships, cars, and trains.

Peter was always stylishly dressed. Thea clearly paid a great deal of attention to his clothes and took obvious delight in his neatness and good looks. Once he had outgrown them, I received the fancy sailor suits and other attractive outfits as hand-me-downs. By contrast, my mother took a very casual attitude regarding my wardrobe. Every spring she bought me a sturdy pair of blue cotton shorts and a few shirts, and I was outfitted for the season. I do not recall my shorts being washed during the entire summer, and I felt very comfortable in my old, rumpled clothes. A snapshot of Peter and me taken at Jurmala in 1930 is characteristic of the differences in our wardrobes. Peter is wearing an elegant knitted suit, socks, and shined shoes. Everything is spotless and neatly pressed. I am in a pair of

Thea and Manfred Peter, Jurmala, 1927.

rumpled shorts and an equally rumpled shirt.

As a Jew, Arthur was dismissed abruptly from his directorship of the factory shortly after the nazi takeover in 1933. He immediately left Germany with Thea and Peter. Arthur's mother, Mutti, had died in Freiburg several years earlier. The Sommerfelds first moved to Paris, where they stayed more than two years. Arthur was unable to find a suitable position, partly because he could not get the coveted Carte de Travail, permission to work in France. Fortuitously, Arthur had been born in Australia and was able to claim British citizenship. Arthur eventually found a position in Birmingham, and the family moved there in 1936. Once in England they changed their name to Summerfield, and Manfred was henceforth known by his middle name Peter.

In England Arthur continued to have difficulty finding a suitable job. He left his first position very shortly and worked intermittently as a consultant, not finding a permanent position until World War II. He worked very hard and put in long hours, but his earnings remained low. After leaving Germany, Arthur was always in difficult financial straits.

The Summerfields' flight from Germany—first to France and later to England—disrupted Peter's schooling. During his stay in Paris he attended a French school. Although he was bright and a good student, he had, I believe, considerable difficulties. After the family moved to Birmingham, Peter started high school in yet another language. His high school records show that after a rocky start, Peter's school performance improved greatly.

Within a year of moving to England, Thea became severely depressed. As her condition worsened, her sister Clara urged her to go to Paris for treatment. Clara, ten years older than Thea, was a strong-willed, determined woman who appeared adamant that Thea stay away from Birmingham. In 1938 Thea entered the Neuro-Psychiatric Clinic of a Dr. Buvat in Paris. On Dr. Buvat's advice she remained in the clinic even after the war started. The decision that Thea remain in Paris was primarily Clara's.

Manfred Peter and me, Jurmala, 1930.

Thea had never worked outside the house, and Peter had been the center of her existence. Her illness and sudden absence must have been another profound disruption in his life. In December 1937 my family sent Paulina Streipa, the practical nurse who had looked after my grandmother, to Birmingham to run the household for Arthur and to look after Peter. Paulina spent the winter of 1937–1938 there. She successfully managed the household and got along well with Peter. Although she liked England, she felt lonely and missed her only daughter. It was decided that despite his mother's illness, Peter would spend his holidays with us as usual. Accordingly, in summer of 1938 Paulina, accompanied by Peter, returned to Riga.

Peter had developed a great interest in classical music and had acquired a remarkable familiarity with classical repertoire. He knew and could recognize many compositions and was able to follow a performance while reading the score. He preferred fast-paced readings and would time each performance and compare the tempi used by different conductors.

Peter could distinguish the individual styles of various conductors and had definite opinions about their interpretations. He was a voracious reader. He amassed a small library and read much Shaw and many other texts.

Our family again requested that Paulina accompany Peter when he returned home, but she would not go because she did not want to leave her daughter. Peter made the return trip home unaccompanied. There was much concern about whether he should stop in Paris where he could visit his mother. In the end he traveled directly to Birmingham. He was not reunited with his mother for more than twelve years.

In December 1938 Arthur signed immigration papers for a Madeleine Goldmann, a refugee from Vienna, to work as a domestic servant in his home. This was one of the few ways of bringing refugees into Britain. Madeleine moved in and took over the household. Arthur was resentful toward Thea's continued absence as well as her illness, which he felt had been a preexisting condition. In 1944, in a letter to Leo, Arthur wrote:

> I cannot conceal the bitterness I feel when I think of the deceptive and
> cruel game played with me before and after my marriage. Every
> physician will tell you that a person once inclined to depressive fits will
> have a relapse sooner or later. All of you were very careful in concealing
> the fact of Thea's illness to me and let me take this appaling risk which
> has now ruined my life.

Leo told me he believed that once Arthur realized that the property in Riga was lost and there was no hope of an inheritance, he lost interest in Thea.

Thea's depression must have lifted, and she left the clinic at the time of the German onslaught on Paris. As I related previously, she escaped from Paris together with Leo and Clara. When Clara refused to continue their flight, Thea joined her in returning to Paris. After the fall of France, Thea remained stranded there for the duration of the German occupation. When Clara was deported by the nazis, Thea survived the war alone in nazi-occupied France. Thea could exhibit great strength when called upon to do so. For more than two years she worked as a housekeeper in a boarding-house in Neuilly, near Paris. She was a British subject, and the nazis did not treat her as a Jew. She was not molested or persecuted in any way.

Communications between occupied France and England had been totally disrupted, and for several years even the Red Cross was unable to provide Arthur with any information as to Thea's whereabouts. Following the liberation of Paris, Thea was repatriated to England where she arrived in December 1944 after an absence of more than seven years. She returned to the house in Birmingham, where Arthur continued to live with Madeleine.

In the summer of 1939 Peter again came to Riga, this time alone. He loved summers at Jurmala, and I think Arthur must have been relieved to send him off, hoping he would have a good vacation. In August Peter came down with colitis, was hospitalized for a couple of weeks, and later spent at least a month in a convalescent home. The outbreak of World War II in September 1939 prevented his return to Birmingham, and he was forced to remain in Riga for more than a year. That winter he was comfortably installed in my grandmother's room, which was next to mine. He did not go to school but studied on his own and tried to keep up with the required curriculum. His interest in music continued, and he started cello lessons. Peter practiced diligently and quickly showed good progress. He occasionally dated the daughter of his mathematics tutor. In summer of 1940, Peter suffered a recurrence of colitis and was again hospitalized for several weeks.

Peter's teenage years were very stressful and, not surprisingly, he became a troubled adolescent. His mother's illness and long absence had a traumatic impact on him. Peter showed great creativity and potential, but he was also difficult and demanding. He demanded books, symphonic scores, and music lessons, and when he received them he would utilize them to great advantage. Increasingly, however, he announced his needs and wants in categorical terms and showed little consideration of others. Uncle Eduard took great interest in him and acted in loco parentis. Eduard liked Peter and thought highly of his talents, but even Eduard found Peter's attitude and insistent demands frustrating.

For my Bar Mitzvah Eduard had given me a modern radio receiver. Before that we had only had a crystal detector radio, a primitive device even by the standards of the day. My new receiver was installed in our library. Peter was able to receive concert broadcasts from Western Europe, which he played at full volume.

As the war progressed it became increasingly clear that Peter would not be able to return to England. In July 1940 the Soviet Union occupied Latvia. England planned the evacuation of its nationals stranded in Riga. Accordingly, in October of that year Peter joined a party of British departing from Riga on the Trans-Siberian railroad to Vladivostok. From there they traveled by boat by way of Shanghai and Hong Kong to Brisbane, Australia. At the end of December 1940, after a two-month journey, Peter landed in Brisbane.

In Brisbane Peter suffered recurrent attacks of ulcerated colitis, and his health remained precarious. He was frequently hospitalized, and several times his condition was considered critical. A scholarship covered his high school tuition, but he was continuously strapped for money. Arthur, himself in a bad financial position, sent Peter as much as he could afford, but it was never enough to cover Peter's expenses. Peter's letters to his father are full of lists of expenses and requests to buy textbooks. Arthur forcefully suggested that Peter find some work to help support himself, but Peter was either unable or unwilling to do so.

After finishing high school, Peter entered college and obtained a full four-year scholarship to study medicine. After the war in Europe had ended, Peter had an opportunity to be repatriated to England. His health made the advisability of the long voyage questionable. There were also questions about interrupting his studies. It was unlikely that Peter would obtain an equivalent scholarship in England. Arthur strongly discouraged Peter from returning, writing that "if you come back now, against my advice, you wont get any allowance from me, and you would have to earn your own keep. I would no longer consent to your living together with me." Peter remained in Brisbane.

Unfortunately, Peter's progress at college was stalled by recurrent attacks of colitis. He was losing weight and had become very weak. In summer of 1950 he had an ileostomy, a procedure long recommended by his doctors. With Leo's financial assistance Thea traveled to Brisbane to help nurse Peter, whose condition was again critical. She rented an apartment and lived there with Peter, who for a time seemed to recover. He dropped the study of medicine but was eventually able to complete a course in science, receiving his bachelor's degree. Again there was talk of his finding a job, but nothing came of it. Peter chose to pursue a one-year honors program that supposedly would give him a chance of securing a better-paying position.

In summer of 1951 Arthur was diagnosed with stomach cancer. His health grew rapidly worse, and he died in September of that year. There was talk of Thea returning to England. In her letters to Leo, Thea spoke bitterly about Arthur and his relationship with Madeleine Goldmann. Madeleine urged Thea to come back to Birmingham, but Thea did not want to do so. In the end, she did not go.

Peter's health continued to deteriorate, and he died in 1953. Thea remained in Brisbane for several more years and finally returned to Birmingham in May 1956. By then she and Madeleine had made their peace, and they lived together in Thea's old house for the remaining years of their lives.

10
Summers at Jurmala

The highlight of our year in Latvia was spending the summer at Jurmala (or Riga Beach), a resort area 15 miles from Riga. Jurmala means "seaside" in Latvian. While my grandmother was alive, it was an annual family reunion. Aunt Thea and Peter regularly spent most of the summer with us, and Arthur joined us for a shorter period. Aunt Clara was also a steady visitor. Uncle Leo dropped by for shorter visits. Uncle Eduard generally preferred to remain in Riga and came to the beach only occasionally.

Jurmala is a long, narrow strip of land between the River Lielupe (called the Aa in German) and the Gulf of Riga. The beach is wide, with pristine, soft white sand and a gentle surf. A string of dunes separates the beach from the villas beyond. In the 1930s the water was crystal clear. Years of Soviet mismanagement have left both the sea and the river badly polluted, and swimming is no longer recommended. Most of the beach had separate morning hours for nude bathing: 8 to 10 A.M. for men and 10:15 to noon for women. No nude bathing was permitted during the afternoons or on weekends, when the beaches were open to both sexes.

Rental accommodations were primitive. The villas had no running water, heat, or bathrooms. We washed in basins in our bedrooms with cold water carried in ceramic or enamel ewers from an outdoor pump. If warm water was desired, it had to be heated on the wood range in the kitchen. There were no laundry facilities; only absolutely necessary laundry was done during the summer.

The absence of washing or laundry facilities did not trouble me. I never considered that my shorts needed washing. My personal hygiene needs were met by the daily swim in the sea and sometimes also in the river. During the summer months showers or baths were unheard of.

At our home there was occasional talk of buying a summer home at the beach, but that was as far as it went. The process of finding a suitable place started about mid-April with repeated resolutions: "Next weekend we must

Michelson family at Jurmala, 1930. Left to right: Manfred Peter, Leo, Thea, Sylvia, Emma, Eduard, Erna, Clara, myself, Arthur, Dietrich.

go and look for a rental villa." We generally procrastinated well into May, at which time the selection of available places was limited. Most years we rented a different place, although sometimes we stayed in the same villa for two years. Jurmala consisted of a number of villages—among them Majori (Majorenhof), Dzintari (Edinburg), Dubulti (Dubeln)—that stretched along the seashore. The more desirable villas were those close to the beach, either just beyond the dunes or within one or two blocks of the beach. We preferred the centrally located Majori-Dzintari area, which had a larger selection of nice villas. There were several small forests nearby, where we would pick wild blueberries and mushrooms.

We moved to the beach in mid-June and back to Riga at the beginning of September. Moving day was full of activity, a day of great excitement for me. The villas were rented furnished, but we brought our own linens, cooking utensils, and dishes. Until the early 1930s these possessions were taken by horse-drawn cart, which took more than half a day to arrive. Later, during the 1930s, the moving was done by truck. I wanted to go with the cart or on the truck but was never allowed to.

Our first order of business after arriving at Jurmala was to register with the police. In Latvia all residents moving to different quarters had to report their new whereabouts within two or three days. The superintendent of each apartment building kept a house book wherein the arrival and departure of all residents were duly recorded. The majority of the house books have survived at the Latvian State Historical Archive and are a valuable source for tracing former inhabitants of Riga.

In the early 1930s my father bought our first car, a Belgian-made, four-door Minerva coupe. My father engaged his young cousin, my namesake Max (Mako) Michelson, then in his mid-twenties, as our chauffeur. The family considered Mako a ne'er-do-well; he had no profession and no steady employment. A great tinkerer, he was interested in automobiles and spent a great deal of time "maintaining" our car, which seemed always to need repairs. At one point my father resolved to learn to drive and started to take lessons from Mako. Mako's tenure as an instructor proved unexpectedly brief. A trip to the beach nearly resulted in disaster: a collision with a peasant's cart. Only pride and the cart sustained significant injury, and my father immediately made good on the damages so as not to be sued. My father was terribly upset and never took another lesson. From then on he left the driving to Mako.

From Jurmala Papa commuted daily by train to work at the factory in Riga—a one-hour trip. Evenings I loved to meet him at the station and walk home with him. Mama went into town only once or twice a week. During the year she worked full-time in the office, but she spent summers mostly at the beach.

Our regular cook, Anna, stayed in Riga, where she kept house for Uncle Eduard. A temporary cook was hired for the summer at the beach. Except for some pickup shopping at the small neighborhood convenience store, all food was bought at the open-air market, and either the cook or our housekeeper, Paulina, made daily trips there.

The market at Jurmala was much smaller than the one in Riga. It consisted of a number of booths and stalls, each of which sold only one kind of product. Thus there were meat, fish, dairy, vegetable, and fruit stalls. During the summer months vegetables and fruits were plentiful, and a good selection of these otherwise scarce products became available. Here, too, everything was displayed on open counters. Even perishable goods, such as meats and fish, were set out uncovered. Only on the hottest days were the perishables surrounded by crushed ice to prevent spoilage.

The market was a lively and fascinating place. Merchants would praise their wares and loudly invite customers to check them out. Their calls were mixed with the cackling and squawking of the poultry. The scents from many products—the sweet smell of butter, the tangy fragrance of smoked fish, the fresh perfume of fruits and berries—all mixed into a tantalizing aroma. Many of these products were delicacies, available in Latvia only during the short summer season. I loved to accompany Paulina on the daily shopping expedition and help her carry home the basket brimming with

Returning from market with Paulina Streipa, Jurmala, 1938.

our purchases.

Smoked fish was a particular specialty in Latvia. We bought these fish directly from fishermen on the beach, who smoked their early morning catch in small shacks right along the beach. The freshly smoked brisling sardines and small flatfish were special delicacies whose freshness and exquisite taste were unsurpassed. The skin would peel away easily and reveal shiny, moist flesh that would literally melt in the mouth. I don't believe I have since tasted any smoked fish as good as that.

When I was smaller I spent most of the day at the beach with my mother or one of my aunts. In the Gulf of Riga the surf was usually gentle, the water was only slightly salty, and the ground fell off very gradually from the shore. It was an ideal place for children to swim and play. One could wade out to the second sandbank without getting into very deep water. I played with Peter, and sometimes my cousin Ali would join us. The one rule, strictly enforced by my parents, was that we were not permitted to go in the water more than once a day, and we had to change into dry bathing suits as soon as we came out of the water. After the swim we would play along the edge of the water, building sand castles, digging holes, and sailing little boats. We would also roam through the dunes, playing hide-and-seek and other games.

During the summer months our cousin Fedya Kretzer and his family

Summer playmates, Jurmala, 1928. Left to right: Myself, Manfred Peter, Ali Kretzer.

also took a villa at Jurmala, usually close to ours. Fedya, the son of my grandmother Emma's sister Tante Minna, was an intimate member of our family circle. His son Alexander (Ali), just ten months my senior, was my closest friend. Ali and I never attended the same schools, but we visited frequently and played together regularly, both in the city and at the beach.

Summer was a time for tennis and swimming lessons. Sylvia took tennis lessons from a stern German pro. I often accompanied Sylvia and acted as her ball boy. Our swimming and diving lessons were given at the Jewish Yacht Club on the River Lielupe by the more amiable Herr Dubrowsky. The arrangements were somewhat primitive. We swam from a small boat dock at the side of the river, and as we progressed, we ventured out farther into the river while Dubrowsky accompanied us in a dory.

After I learned to swim, I enjoyed going out to the third sandbank and even a bit beyond it. Between the second and third sandbanks the water was deep, well over my head. Except for stormy days in late August, the sea was usually calm, there was no undertow, and it was fairly safe to swim out to the third sandbank. There were no lifeguards, however, and one had to use common sense.

Later, when I had a bike, I became much more independent. No longer limited to the confines of our villa, I moved freely all over Jurmala. Several of my high school classmates also spent summers at Jurmala, and my social life became very busy. In 1939, which was to be my last summer at the beach, I joined the Jewish tennis club, Ritek. We played at the club, and afterward we hung out at the local ice cream parlor. We went on bike outings and had impromptu parties. It was a particularly enjoyable summer. Oblivious to the gathering clouds of war, I had a marvelous time.

11
My Schools

The course of my education was strongly influenced by the political events in Latvia. School was divided into a seven-year elementary school followed by a five-year high school. For me as for many of my friends, the orderly progression through elementary and high school was repeatedly unsettled by changes not only in schools but also by abrupt shifts in the language of instruction. During my ten years of schooling in Riga I attended three schools and was taught in four different languages: German, Latvian, Hebrew, and Russian. Switching to a new school or changing the language of instruction was always stressful. I was afraid of finding myself in an unaccustomed and possibly difficult situation.

As a result of the frequent changes in the language of instruction, I studied many languages but did not master any of them. German was my first language, and I am fluent in it, although my formal German studies ended in second grade. Having completed a Latvian elementary school, my command of Latvian had been good, but I have not retained fluency. I can still read Latvian text; however, I can follow and understand only the most elementary conversations. I surmise that, considering my dislike of things Latvian, this memory lapse may have a psychological basis. I never became fluent in either Russian or Hebrew. My formal Russian studies, although intensive, lasted only one year. I acquired a passable vocabulary and learned to write elementary essays, but I did not become proficient. My Hebrew lessons at school reinforced the knowledge gained during private lessons at home. Hebrew was taught only during my first two years of high school; the lessons stopped after the Soviet annexation of Latvia. Lack of practice and a limited vocabulary have again kept me from achieving competency.

There were no public kindergartens, and at age six I went to a small private one. I have little recollection of it. The following fall I started pre-school in a German-language public elementary school. I spent three years at the German school, attending through second grade. The school was coed, and many of the children in my grade were Jewish. I made a number of friends among my fellow Jewish students. The instruction was entirely in German, and I learned to write using the Gothic script.

As has been mentioned, in May 1934, just as I was finishing second grade, Latvian prime minister Karlis Ulmanis, supported by his Peasant Party and a paramilitary militia, the Aizsargi (Home Guards), executed a coup. A state of emergency was declared, the Saims was dissolved, and political parties were banned. Ulmanis became president and thenceforth ruled by decree. One of Ulmanis's earliest decrees directed that children attend

Ready for elementary school with my green uniform cap, 1931.

either a Latvian school or a school of their own ethnic background. The new nationalistic regime was extremely hostile to the country's ethnic minorities—mainly Russians, Germans, and Jews—who constituted a significant segment of Latvia's population. Reducing the educational autonomy of minorities reflected the government's desire to circumscribe minority rights in general.

The new regulation meant I was not permitted to continue my education at the German school. The options available were either a Latvian or a Jewish school. My parents favored a Jewish school. Many Jewish schools in Riga, mostly private, offered instruction in Yiddish, Hebrew, or German. Now that German was officially no longer an acceptable language for Jewish children, the German-language Jewish schools had to switch to Hebrew, Yiddish, or, in theory anyway, Latvian. Given my family's attitude, Yiddish was out of the question, and a Jewish school therefore meant a Hebrew-language school. Unfortunately, there was no Hebrew school near our home, so it was decided that I should attend the public Latvian Kronvalda (23rd) elementary school, which was within easy walking distance.

I started third grade at the Latvian elementary school in fall of 1934. I remember this period vividly, as I found several aspects of the new school worrisome. Instruction was in Latvian, a language I was not comfortable with. What little Latvian I knew was mostly acquired by talking with our cook, Anna. What really troubled me was writing. At the German school I had learned to write using Gothic script. Now at the Latvian school I was expected to use Latin script. I saw this as a challenge to my newly acquired writing skills. The fact that several of my Jewish classmates also transferred to the same Latvian school made the unfamiliar situation a little less scary.

The school had three parallel third-grade classes: A, B, and C. Classes A and B, for boys and girls, respectively, had no Jewish students. Class C was coed and had been formed the year I entered to accommodate the sudden influx of Jewish children. Almost half of my class of twenty-seven students was Jewish. My contact with students in the A and B classes was minimal.

Once, when I was alone in the boys' room, I was cornered by several older boys who made anti-Semitic remarks. Although I managed to slip away without further trouble, I was shaken by the incident.

We attended school six days a week, half a day on Saturdays. The whole class had the same schedule. There were five or six periods per day. Except for gym and science labs, we stayed in our homeroom and teachers for the different subjects came to us. We did not have any study or free periods during school hours. We were dismissed at 3:00, and I got home just in time for the main meal of the day at 3:30 P.M.

The students in my class at the elementary school remained together for four years. I developed close friendships with my Jewish classmates, some of which have lasted a lifetime. Our homeroom teacher for those four years was Ozolinya kundze, whom I came to know very well. (Kundze is the Latvian address for Mrs. It is an honorific meaning *lady* and is placed after the name.) Ozolinya kundze was an ordained Lutheran minister and taught religion at our school. Jewish students were excused from religion class but were permitted to remain in the room. I had no homework and was not called on in class, but I enjoyed listening to the Bible stories.

Ozolinya was a soft-spoken, kind, and friendly person; I felt comfortable with and was fond of her. When my friend Thea met her in Riga after the war, Ozolinya inquired as to the whereabouts of her former students.

My other elementary school teachers made a less favorable impression on me than my homeroom teacher. None of them was Jewish, and for the most part they seemed cold and unapproachable. I remember only two by name: Plaucinya, who taught science or mathematics, and Petersone, who taught Latvian. I had practically no contact with our principal, Sprivulis kungs (the Latvian address for Mr., literally meaning *sir*). I have heard that he was a Social Democrat and supposedly a very decent person.

Other than signing my report cards, my parents were little involved in my day-to-day school activities. There were few, if any, parent-teacher conferences, and my mother seldom, if ever, came to the school. I was a good student and knew my parents expected it of me. My report cards were always good, and my mother did not find it necessary to see my teachers.

In our elementary school all students were required to wear uniforms. Girls wore dark-blue skirts and white blouses; boys had military-style, black wool tunics and long pants. One did not wear a shirt under the tunic, but a white collar band was basted inside the tunic so a narrow white edge showed along the neck. Once a week we had a military education class, devoted mostly to marching drills but also to rifle range instruction. Our instructor regularly inspected the condition of our uniforms, and I made sure I had pressed my pants and sewn in a clean collar for his class.

At the Latvian elementary school Jewish boys were expected to attend after-hours Jewish religious classes. We did not take the class seriously and behaved like hooligans. The poor teacher was unable to enforce any kind of discipline. He did not want to report us to the principal because that would reflect on his performance as a teacher. He also felt it was behavior unbecoming for Jewish boys. We took terrible advantage of the poor man. Needless to say, I did not learn anything in these classes.

In May 1935 my school took part in a citywide nationalistic celebration on the anniversary of the Ulmanis takeover. Under the direction of our gym teacher, we had been practicing Latvian folk dancing. Garbed in the traditional Latvian folk costume, I participated in the mass dance presentation at the local sports stadium. Although some of the students, particularly the girls, had elaborate costumes, I wore the minimum that could pass as an ethnic outfit: plain gray unbleached linen pants tied at the ankles and a simple white linen shirt without ornamentation. I went through the steps mechanically, without any enthusiasm. I must have contributed little to the overall quality of our presentation. My disdain for folk dancing can probably be traced to this less-than-positive experience.

I had only casual contacts and did not develop any real friendships with my non-Jewish classmates. I was not asked to their homes and did not invite them to mine. One of my Latvian classmates kept pigeons in a little shack in an area of community gardens. I occasionally accompanied him and watched him release the pigeons. After a brief flight they always returned to the coop. I found these visits fascinating. Once my classmate complimented me: "For a Jew you are all right." I resented his attitude and lost interest in pigeons.

After finishing the Latvian elementary school in 1938, I had to choose a high school. Once again the choice was between a Latvian public high school and a private Jewish school. Like my Jewish classmates I was apprehensive at the prospect of attending a Latvian school where the atmosphere, if not overtly anti-Semitic, was hardly friendly. We did not feel welcome there. None of my Jewish classmates elected to enroll in a Latvian school.

The choices of Jewish schools were varied. Some Jewish schools offered instruction in Hebrew or Yiddish or some combination of these with Latvian. My parents preferred the Ezra Schule, a private Jewish high school with a reputation for educational excellence, which catered to assimilationist elements in the Jewish population. I was agreeable, and that fall I entered Ezra School.

German had originally been the primary language at Ezra School. By edict of the Ulmanis government, the school had officially shifted to a combination of Hebrew and Latvian. My classmates' and my own competency in Hebrew was limited, as was that of many of our teachers, and in practice German continued to be used in several subjects.

Using its influence at the Ministry of Education, Agudat Israel had pushed regulations to make the Jewish schools more religiously observant. Holding classes on the Sabbath was not permitted, and we had a half-day of instruction on Sunday mornings rather than on Saturdays. I considered this objectionable at first but soon adjusted to it. Daily attendance at morning minyan was obligatory for boys, necessitating our arrival at the school about twenty minutes prior to the start of classes. During the morning service boys, who had been Bar Mitzvah, were expected to put on tefillin (phylacteries).

The principal of Ezra School was Herr Löwenstamm, a strict disciplinarian. He was nicknamed Grintz, meaning "grin" or "smirk," referring to the grim smile perpetually frozen on his face. Herr Löwenstamm was a pedantic man, and he insisted that all our writing be done on unlined paper. Herr Löwenstamm was demanding but fair so that although not liked, he was respected.

The school's physical facilities were inadequate. The school occupied several floors of a five-story apartment building that was also the home of our principal. The classrooms were undersized, usually consisting of adjacent rooms whose common wall had been removed. Our classroom was long and narrow and had an odd-shaped protrusion at its center. There was barely enough space for desks for all the students. We did not have a proper gym or an assembly hall that could accommodate the entire student body. The school clearly depended on tuition payments for its survival. There was a single class in each grade, and the total enrollment in the five high school grades could not have exceeded 150.

There were about thirty students in my class my first year at the high school, and over the three years that I attended Ezra School I became good friends with many of them. One of my closest friends was Michael (Mika) Löwenstamm, the son of our principal. He was a good student; he knew he had to do well, or his father would have made his life miserable.

As in elementary school, our entire class had the same course schedule. Our only choice was whether to take French or Latin. I opted for French, which was taught by Madame Golodyetz, a diminutive middle-aged lady. Madame Golodyetz conducted her class entirely in French, and she gave me a good foundation.

Our English teacher was Herr Ribofsky, who also taught Latin. He was very strict and maintained excellent decorum in his classes. Herr Ribofsky's English pronunciation was notoriously poor, but he more than made up for it with a well-organized approach and an emphasis on vocabulary and grammar. In three years under his rigorous tutelage, I gained reasonable fluency in the language. Algebra, a subject I liked and in which I excelled, was taught by our principal, Herr Löwenstamm.

During my first year in high school I took ballroom dancing lessons with one of our teachers, Frau von Wildeman, a big, well-endowed, and exuberant woman. She encouraged the boys to lead and, while dancing with me, invariably insisted that I hold her firmly and closely.

Many high school students belonged to the youth groups of various Jewish political organizations. Several were members of Betar, the youth arm of the Revisionists, and others belonged to the left-wing Hashomer Hatzair. There were no religious youth groups in my school because children from religious families did not attend Ezra School. Several fraternities, modeled on their college counterparts, were also active. Members of these fraternities attempted to emulate the behavior of college students in both drinking and womanizing—or at least in bragging about it. A few of my friends were members of SK (Studenten Korporation), one of the fraternities. My family, particularly Uncle Eduard, disapproved of the pervasive drinking and carousing and condemned the aims of fraternities in general and the behavior of fraternity brothers in particular. Strongly influenced by these opinions, I never considered joining a fraternity.

12
Soviet Occupation of Latvia

During the summer of 1940, just prior to the Soviet annexation of Latvia, I went to work on a farm for an obligatory four-week term. Germany's attack on Poland had caused a shortage of imported farm labor, and the Ulmanis regime decided to mobilize high school and university students, boys and girls age fifteen and older, to help bring in the harvest. My father arranged for me to do my stint at a farm named Kauļi (Latvian for "bones") near Jekabpils, about two hours from Riga by train. The parents of some of my friends paid the farmers for taking them, but I do not think my father did. My friends reported that for them the four-week work period was more like summer camp.

The farmer treated me well, and we became friendly. Seeing me as a city kid not accustomed to the rigors of farm life, he indulged me a bit. I was not made to get up with the rest of the household at about 4 A.M. but was allowed to sleep until breakfast at 7 A.M. Otherwise, I put in a full day's work and was treated like just another farmhand. The farm owned no tractors; everything was done with horses. I learned both to harness them and to use the horse-drawn machinery such as hay cutters, reapers, and horse rakes. The farm had about 75 acres and a dozen cows, and it grew wheat, rye, barley, oats, and potatoes. I found the work varied and interesting and enjoyed the experience. I also liked the hardy diet: sour-grass soup with thick slabs of bacon for breakfast and rich soups with homemade black bread and plenty of butter for the main meals.

While I was on the farm the political situation in Latvia was deteriorating rapidly. The Soviet Union demanded additional military bases on Latvian territory. Within days, by July 17, 1940, the Red Army had occupied the entire country and deposed the Ulmanis regime. We followed the events by radio, listening with disbelief as the communist propaganda broadcasts reported widespread popular rejoicing at being freed from the fascist regime. Particularly galling to my host were reports describing the liberation of enslaved farm laborers from the clutches of rich farmers. Special note was made of how these scoundrels sexually exploited women workers. This accusation provoked some teasing of the farmer by both his wife and the other females on the farm. A week later, having completed my four weeks on the farm, I returned to the new reality in Riga.

Following the Soviet annexation of Latvia, a dramatic change of emphasis occurred in the courses and curricula taught in the schools. The language of instruction was changed to Russian. Hebrew was eliminated completely, and Latvian was taught only as a language course. Also eliminated was any religious observance, including the morning minyan.

The Communist Party must have considered Ezra School a hotbed of bourgeois opposition, and indoctrination in Marxism-Leninism became our most important subject. The course was taught by an old-time party member, a graduate of the previously outlawed underground communist movement in Latvia. He was a humorless man who came to class with a gun bulging conspicuously in his outside jacket pocket. The course covered fundamentals of Marxism and Leninism and included readings from Marx, Engels, and Lenin. Most important, it included *A Short Course of the Communist Party of Bolsheviks,* the bible of the new state religion, and I quickly became adept at writing essays in Russian that regurgitated and paraphrased the Stalinist gospel.

For me, the year under the new Soviet regime was a time of conflicting emotions. On the one hand, I witnessed and was victimized by the persecution of our family as "members of the bourgeoisie." Our property was expropriated, and my father lost his position and had great difficulty finding another job, even a marginally suitable one. My mother stopped working in the office at the factory and became a full-time housewife. Forced to leave our house, we moved to a two-bedroom apartment in Mežaparks, which could accommodate only a small portion of our furniture and belongings. We took my parents' bedroom set, the dining room set, and the piano. All of the rest was left in our former home. Our house contained a considerable number of Leo's artworks. My father tried the best he could to save these paintings and a few other belongings by moving them into a small, dilapidated shack on the only one of our properties that remained in our possession.

On the other hand, I found high school exciting. We were treated more like adults and asked to participate in political activities. I was aware that it was all propaganda, but it was still a heady time. I was sixteen years old and for the first time in my life was invited to participate in a political process. During the Ulmanis dictatorship all political activity was forbidden; we were taught what to say and think and that it was best not to do too much of either. Now we still had to toe a party line, but we were invited—

actually directed—to participate, and that appealed to my self-importance. The truth was that in school the Soviets tried hard to indoctrinate us, and their efforts were not subtle. There were many extracurricular activities. We met, we talked, we planned, yet all of it was a sham. I knew the reality of the Soviet regime was shockingly different from the rosy, optimistic propaganda, but active participation in school life was a novelty, and it was exciting.

Early in fall of 1940 our school had to help bring in the potato harvest. One weekend about thirty teenagers and several teacher chaperons took a train to a farm about an hour's ride from Riga. The work was hard, we had to stoop constantly to pick potatoes, and we did not do a good job—a lot of the potatoes remained unpicked. Our overnight stay was great fun, however. We slept on mattresses on the floor in a couple of rooms. The boys were in the larger back room, and the girls were in the smaller one in front. During the night some mingling of boys and girls occurred. The highlight of the evening was Herr Ribofsky telling ribald tales about Madame Golodyetz, our French teacher. I do not know whether the potato harvest was a success, but the trip was a great adventure for us.

My classmates Mika Löwenstamm and Lyuba Treskunoff lived in Mežaparks, the suburb where my family had our new apartment. Having lost their apartment at Ezra School, the Löwenstamms had also recently moved here, and their place was just around the corner from where I lived. Lyuba's family lived in a comfortable villa one block away. We used to take the trolley to and from school together and would also meet afternoons and evenings. I saw a lot of Lyuba. I used to help her with algebra, a subject she found difficult. When the weather was nice, we would go for strolls in the nearby woods.

Saturday evening, June 7, 1941, we had a party at Leo Sokolowitch's apartment to celebrate the end of our school year. About half of our class was there. I did not know it at the time, but it was our last big event before the war started. The party was a great success, with lots of dancing and drinking. It lasted into the early morning hours. In Riga streetcars and buses stopped running after midnight. I remember sitting with Lyuba and Bubi Fried at the bus terminal at six o'clock on a bright Sunday morning waiting for the first bus to Mežaparks. During the war years I clung to the memory of that party and my friends. The thought that after the war we would meet and celebrate again was a great encouragement during the darkest hours.

During the Soviet occupation Mika Löwenstamm joined the Komsomol, the communist youth organization. We spent many long evenings in political discussions. Edith Nathanson, a former classmate who had emigrated to the United States just prior to the Soviet takeover, wrote complaining about life in New York. Her unhappiness and the relative merits of life in a capitalist country versus the Soviet Union became the topic of heated debates. Mika defended the party line. He praised the Soviet Union and denigrated life in the Western democracies. With Mika I still felt free to voice my true feelings about our new regime. I believed Edith's unhappiness was the result of her personal situation, not a reflection on capitalism. Shortly after coming to New York City in 1947 I saw Edith on several occasions, but we did not hit it off very well. Our final break resulted from a trivial incident. She and another former classmate were in my apartment when we decided to prepare dinner. She insisted on making hamburgers and wanted to add milk to the meat. Both my friend and I objected vehemently. During the ensuing argument I told her she did not know how to make hamburgers, and I made them myself, without any milk. Edith was very insulted. It was the last time I saw her. In retrospect, I still could not get over my irritation at those letters describing how unhappy she was in New York and how difficult she found life in the United States.

During the night of June 13 and into the early morning hours of June 14, the NKVD rounded up many prominent civilians and their families for deportation to the interior of the Soviet Union. The lists of deportees, prepared by the NKVD, included local businessmen, members of Jewish Zionist organizations such as Betar, Jewish student fraternities, and many others. This was done ostensibly to remove the bourgeoisie and other "unreliable elements" from the border regions with Germany. Following a midnight knock on the door, people were given just half an hour to pack one small valise and, loaded into cattle cars, were shipped to unknown destinations.

Although many friends and acquaintances were picked up that night, our family was not taken. For the next few days we slept with our suitcases packed, and every morning we awoke relieved that we had not been picked up. During breakfast and dinner we talked about who had been deported. There was much speculation as to why some people had been taken but others were not. We felt greatly comforted that somehow we had been spared. It was to be a short-lived comfort. My family's recent change of apartments, the move to Mežaparks, probably saved us from deportation. Regardless of the horrendous conditions in Soviet camps, however, chances of survival were still better there than under the nazis. The unprecedented brutality of the deportation confirmed my family's loathing of the Stalinist regime and discouraged any thought we might have had of trying to escape ahead of the German occupation. The fact that my close friends had become victims of the deportation brought me to a startling realization. We had thought of ourselves as potential victims of nazi Germany. Despite our material losses we had been prepared to join the Soviet Union in the fight against the common adversary. But now, suddenly, the Soviets were treating Jews in the Baltic countries as security risks and potential enemies.

About 40,000 people were deported from Latvia, including at least 5,000 Jews.[14] We thought the high number of Jewish deportees reflected the anti-Semitism of the Latvian communists in charge of preparing the deportation lists. (The Latvians, in turn, blamed the deportations on Jewish communists.) Among those taken were my classmate and friend Harry Baum and the host of our big party, Leo Sokolowitch.

The men deported from Riga in June 1941 were separated from their families and sent to camps in far northern European Russia, west of the Urals. The conditions in these camps were terrible—famine, bitter cold, and hard labor—and almost everyone sent there perished. Women and children were sent into exile in middle Asia, typically Kazakhstan, where most survived. Among the survivors was Leo Sokolowitch. Leo died soon after the war, however, of a brain tumor. Harry Baum also survived the war in the Soviet Union and, after spending many years in the Gulag, he returned to Riga. In the late 1970s he was able to emigrate to Israel.

PART II
The War and Postwar Years

We recall with grief all Your children who have perished through the cruelty of the oppressor, victims of demonic hate: the aged and young, the learned and unlettered—all driven in multitudes along the road of pain and pitiless death. Their very presence on earth was begrudged them, for they brought Your covenant of mercy and justice to the recollection of your enemies; they perished because they were a symbol of Your eternal law; their death has brought darkness to the human soul.

They lie in nameless graves, in far-off forests and lonely fields. And the substance of many was scattered by the winds to the earth's four corners. Yet they shall not be forgotten. We take them into our hearts and give them a place beside the cherished memories of our own beloved ones.

—FROM THE MEMORIAL SERVICE LITURGY

13

Germany Attacks the Soviet Union

In the early morning hours of Sunday, June 22, 1941, Germany attacked the Soviet Union. Stalin and the Red Army were caught totally by surprise, and the precipitous retreat of the Red Army almost immediately became a rout. The previous week I had started a summer job at a furniture factory, but the factory closed within a couple of days after the start of the war. During the days following the attack I witnessed endless columns of trucks carrying Red Army soldiers driving east through town. It was a time of general confusion; rumors were rampant.

Shortly after the war started, the local authorities organized an air raid warden service. The residents of each apartment building had to arrange for a rotating guard assignment during the evening and night hours. The warden was to stay in the front yard, watch for enemy planes, and alert the residents in case of an air attack or fire. I spent one night on duty from 2 A.M. to 6 A.M. It was a starry, chilly night. Nothing happened; I found myself bored and very cold because I was not dressed appropriately. I considered the assignment important and took my duties seriously.

The Soviets discouraged the general population from escaping before the nazi onslaught. The people of Latvia were considered untrustworthy and were not given an opportunity to flee the advancing German army. A number of German and Austrian Jews who had sought refuge from the nazis in Latvia, however, were deported to Siberia. Among them was my classmate Armin (Bubi) Fried and his family. The Communist Party evacuated its members, often in a precipitous manner. The father of one family returned to his apartment in the middle of the day to pick up his wife and children. They had only one hour to catch the truck leaving from his place of employment. Their older son was sick and had stayed home, but his five-year-old brother was at nursery school. In the confusion the parents were unable to locate their younger son and were forced to flee to Russia without him. They were never able to trace the boy or to discover what happened to him.

A similar story is told by two sisters Zeitlin, classmates of my friend Max Gutkin. Their father, working in a local bank, was able to arrange for a truck to take the family to the Soviet Union. He sent the truck to pick up his two daughters, with the understanding that it would then return to get him and his wife so the entire family could escape together. The truck picked up the girls at their home and immediately left Riga, leaving the parents stranded. The two sisters survived, but their parents were killed during the liquidation of the Riga Ghetto.

My friend Mika Löwenstamm also fled to the Soviet Union. In late June, a few days after the war started, I spent the afternoon with Mika. He gave no hint of planning to escape from Riga. When I came to see him the next day I found only his distraught mother. Mika had left with the Komsomol for Russia on less than an hour's notice and with barely so much as a good-bye. He probably did not know about the evacuation plans until the last minute. When the opportunity to escape presented itself, he, like many others, decided on the spur of the moment to run.

My parents and Uncle Eduard discussed the possibility of escaping, perhaps using our car, which despite having been requisitioned was still available. The Red Army was offering no resistance and was clearly abandoning Riga to the Germans. The prospect of living under the nazis was terrifying. We knew about the earlier persecutions of the Jews in Germany and Poland. We expected a brutal regime, vicious oppression, possibly even pogroms. The thought that Germany would embark on a state-sponsored and state-organized killing of the entire Jewish population, however, never entered our minds. Arguing against a successful escape were rumors that Latvian partisans were intercepting and killing refugees on the highways leading to the Soviet Union. Furthermore, the former border between Latvia and the Soviet Union was said to be closed. In the end we elected to stay in Riga. It is interesting to note that in 1915, during World War I, when Riga was about to fall to the German army, the entire family (Emma, Clara, Eduard, Thea, and my parents) escaped to Moscow, where they spent the remaining war years. The fact that Russia was now ruled by the Soviets, as well as the still fresh memory of the recent deportations, weighed heavily in our decision to stay.

I often think with regret about our not taking the nazi threat more seriously and fleeing to the Soviet Union. I do not blame my parents for that decision. It was clearly my responsibility to decide for myself, but I did not yet perceive myself as capable of independent action. In a sense I saw myself as a child, bound by the decision of the entire family. The very suddenness with which the situation developed and the need to act decisively, almost impulsively, worked against my leaving. Ultimately, I can blame only myself. Several of my classmates did leave Riga without their parents, although in most cases they were accompanying an older sibling.

Our decision was not unusual. Professor Vladimir Mintz, the famous Riga surgeon, is quoted as saying "the Russians have already taken my house and my car. What can I expect from them if I escape to the Soviet Union?" Ten days after his pronouncement, on July 1, 1941, Riga fell to the German troops, and the fate of the Jews remaining in Riga was sealed. Professor Mintz went through the Large and the Little Ghettos in Riga and the Kaiserwald concentration camp and died in 1944 in Buchenwald.

Most of the people who had escaped from Riga just prior to the German occupation survived the war in the Soviet Union. Many of the younger men were drafted into the Red Army, and some were killed in the war. The conditions during the war were very difficult and life was hard, but as difficult as it was, it was paradise compared to the nazi camps. At that time the Soviets were not overtly anti-Semitic. Campaigns against Zionism and "cosmopolitanism" (the latter was a code word for identifying Jews) did not become part of Soviet policy until the late 1940s.

My classmate Mika Löwenstamm survived the war and became a medical doctor. He worked as a hematologist in a research institute in the Ukraine. Mika died in the late 1950s as a result of contracting some exotic disease. I lost track of Mika's parents and do not know whether they were in the Riga Ghetto or were seized from their apartment and killed during the early days of the occupation.

The interval between the Soviet retreat and the German occupation of Riga was ominously quiet. No street fighting occurred, and the Red Army had been gone for several days, but the Germans had not yet arrived. The only evidence of warfare was some sporadic shelling of the downtown area. The gilded rooster on top of the tall steeple of Saint Peter's Church was a prominent landmark of Riga's skyline. Now I saw the steeple erupt in flames and tumble below the horizon. Our suburb of Mežaparks remained serene. For us it proved to be the proverbial quiet before the storm.

14

The Nazis Enter Riga

The nazi invasion of the Soviet Union marked the beginning of a new phase of World War II, one that brought the hostilities to our doorstep. German army units did not actually enter Riga until July 1, 1941. In the Jewish community it is generally believed that the attacks on the Jews started even before the nazis' arrival, although Marger Vesterman, a Jewish historian now working in Riga, has been unable to find any documentary evidence of attacks on Jews prior to the nazi occupation. There was a great deal of confusion at the time, so the difference in our perception of these events is not surprising. Also not terribly surprising is the silence of the Latvian auxiliaries who perpetrated these outrages. These murderers were certainly not eager to leave any record of their crimes.

The attacks involved members of Perkonkrusts, the Latvian nazi party; Aizsargi, the revived pre-Soviet-period fascist paramilitary militia; and students from Latvian fraternities, as well as local thugs and hoodlums. On July 1 the local radio station broadcast an appeal for all patriotic Latvians to join the battle against the internal enemy, namely the Jews. According to the anti-Semitic propaganda, all Jews were communists, and all Soviet functionaries were Jews. Jews were to blame for the Soviet occupation of Latvia, particularly for the Soviet-era victimization and deportation of Latvians. In fact, ethnic Latvian communists had supplied many of the Soviet cadres for the government of Latvia.[15] Having failed to resist the Soviet occupation, the Latvians needed little encouragement to become convinced that they had been betrayed by the Jews.

The Latvian volunteers were issued guns and red-and-white armbands and were assigned to "work" in specific precincts.[16] The assaults grew into full-scale pogroms, with random killings, rapes, tortures, and looting. Jews were seized in the streets or dragged from their apartments. Many were taken to police headquarters, the Prefecture, in the center of Riga to be taunted, tortured, raped, and killed. Under the chaotic conditions prevailing at that time, some men were not killed immediately but were thrown into Central Prison, while women were taken to Terminka Prison.

On July 4, 1941, several hundred Jews from apartment buildings in the immediate neighborhood were herded into the Great Choral Synagogue on Gogol iela (street), where they perished when the building was set ablaze. Five of the six large Riga synagogues were torched that week with people locked inside. The destruction was not limited to synagogues. Chapels on the grounds of Riga's two Jewish cemeteries were burned to the ground with the rabbis, their families, and Jews from the vicinity locked inside. The smaller houses of prayer, the minyanim, were all destroyed in similar fashion. Only the Peitavas Street synagogue, our family's place of worship in the densely built-up old city, was spared. Its proximity to surrounding buildings meant it could not be burned without incinerating much of the old city of Riga. Later the Germans gutted it and turned it into a storehouse, but the building did not suffer serious structural damage. After the war the Holy Ark was discovered intact behind the boarded-up eastern wall. So hidden, it had escaped desecration. The Peitavas Street synagogue has since been restored, and today it is the sole operating synagogue in Riga.

Although the city was firmly under the control of the German army, no effort was made to curtail the violence against the Jews. To the contrary, the nazis gave the local Latvian paramilitary units free rein. According to the SS, the pogroms were a spontaneous manifestation of Latvian hatred of the Jews. The voluntary police and the Perkonkrusts were encouraged to proceed with the elimination of the Jews. The Latvians continued their haphazard attacks on the Jewish community. They pulled Jews, mostly men, from their apartments. Among those arrested were prominent community leaders: physicians, attorneys, and businessmen. Most were killed immediately, but some were taken to Central Prison, which remained under the control of Latvian units. The majority of those taken to prison were also killed.[17] Only some doctors were later released.

The fate that befell two old friends of our family is typical of what happened to many Jews in Riga during the days following the arrival of the Germans. Otto Sachs, the director of a Riga cement factory, lived in the Riga suburb Agenskalns. He and his family had been thrown out of their home after it was requisitioned by German army officers. The Sachs family managed to find refuge in the nearby apartment of Otto's brother-in-law, attorney Alfons Heideman. Late at night on July 21, the two men were taken from the apartment by two armed Latvians. The following morning they were found shot to death in nearby woods.

In early July my cousin Ali Kretzer was seized from his apartment for a work detail. He returned home that evening under strict instructions to report again the next morning. Against his mother's advice he went back the next day, confident that he was reporting for more work. He was never seen or heard from again. Like most of the Jews ostensibly taken to work, he was killed in one of the nearby forests.

My longtime friend and elementary school classmate Max Gutkin was living with his parents and brothers in his father's large apartment building at the corner of Brivibas and Matisa iela, a centrally located, prosperous area. One evening a Latvian who was a tenant in the building appeared at the service entrance of the Gutkins' apartment and warned Max's father to get away at once. The tenant seemed extremely nervous and left abruptly. The Gutkins spent the night hidden in the coal cellar. Cautiously returning the next morning, they found their front door smashed in. The apartment had been ransacked, but nothing was taken. It had evidently been searched for its inhabitants.

As has been mentioned, our family home, along with the factory, had been nationalized by the new Soviet government the previous November. My parents and I had moved to Mežaparks and lived in a small apartment in a five-unit building. We were the only Jews and had not yet become acquainted with our neighbors. Ironically, the fact that we were not known in that area in all likelihood saved us from being arrested and killed during the first days of the occupation. That was only a temporary reprieve.

Shortly after the German occupation began, I went to the furniture factory in the hope of getting my job back. At first I was advised to check again in a couple of days, but upon returning I was told there was no work for me and not to come back.

Anxious and restless, without a job to occupy me, I could not sit still or even stay in our apartment during the day. I took to roaming the streets and the nearby woods, never coming home before dinnertime. For a week that was my routine. On the eighth day, when I returned my mother was gone. "She should be home very soon," Papa said. The Latvian volunteer police had come to take him off to work. He was not well, however, and Mama had prevailed on them to allow her to go in his place. She did not return that evening or the next day. I never saw her or heard from her again. My father made inquiries and heard she was in prison. He clung to that report. He may even have received several messages he assumed to be from her. If indeed she was taken to prison, she was killed there later. After the war I learned that about 1,500 Jewish women had been brought to Terminka Prison at that time. The women were eventually taken to the nearby Bikernieku forest and murdered; none survived. It did not occur to me at the time that had I been home I almost certainly would have been taken. Not until years after liberation did I appreciate how accidental my survival that day had been.

The horror and incomprehensible cruelty of the pogroms affected people in different ways. Some chose to take their own lives, and several families took poison. They probably concluded they had little or no chance of survival, and the prospect of separation was more terrible than death. Only about 1 percent of the Latvian Jews eventually survived the war, and those who did were disproportionately male. For women, children, and the elderly, the chances of survival were substantially poorer. The majority of people clung to life, however. Placing hope upon hope, we found reasons to be optimistic even where there were none. We discounted the attacks as a local aberration resulting from the transfer of power and looked forward to a normalization and stabilization of our situation. Such is the power of wishful thinking that we continued to perceive the ongoing brutality perpetrated against the Jewish community as a murderous initiative on the part of the numerous Latvian fascists. We not only hoped, we actually expected that once installed, the German civil authorities would suppress what we naively concluded were spontaneous, unauthorized attacks. It was assumed that the conditions imposed on us would be harsh, but we nevertheless expected some measure of order and stability. It was inconceivable that the Germans, even the nazi regime, would systematically pursue a policy aimed at annihilating the entire Jewish population. (The word *genocide* had not been coined.) Germany was a bastion of Western civilization and culture. We admired German cultural and technological achievements; we were proud to speak German at home.

In late July 1941 the city came under a German civil administration. The new authorities included many Germans of Baltic origin who had been repatriated to Germany in 1939 and who now returned to govern what they believed was rightfully their country. Among the German Balts virulent anti-Semitism was the norm. Their dedication and commitment to "solving the Jewish problem" and the energy they displayed in pursuit of that goal outdid even the Gestapo in some cases.

There was some reason for hope that our situation would improve under the civil administration. But in August 1941 an edict was issued that all Jews must move into a ghetto. Once there, instead of the civil administration, we came under the direct control of the Gestapo and the SS (Schutzstaffel, German for *protection squad,* paramilitary elite nazi units used as police and concentration camp staff). Members of the SS rarely indicated any support or empathy for the Jews. But in contacts with soldiers and officers of the Wehrmacht (German army), one occasionally met decent individuals who would express disagreement with nazi policies. Stories of such encounters circulated among us and helped to sustain our wishful belief that opposition to Hitler existed. Max Gutkin relates how in late fall of 1941, together with a small group of Jews from the Riga Ghetto, he did maintenance work in a building housing a German army communications outfit. One day the commanding officer of the unit, who had never taken notice of his Jewish workers, stormed through the building deploring its filthy condition. "You dirty Jews! You will stay here all night and make sure the place is cleaned up," he screamed. Accordingly, the work detail was detained and prevented from returning to the ghetto that evening. The liquidation of the ghetto began that night. The officer apparently felt the safest way to protect his Jewish workers was to make a public display of anti-Semitism.

However sincere such individuals may have been, these were at best isolated occurrences. Even if they were sympathetic to the plight of the Jews, most soldiers did not act on their decent impulses. A pervasive and well-founded fear of the Gestapo kept most sympathetically inclined Germans from offering any tangible help. Army units almost always contained at least a few fanatical nazis. These zealots would try to ensure that no common courtesy, no correct behavior, let alone any assistance was extended to any Jew. Fellow officers or soldiers observed to perform such acts were speedily denounced. The usual punishment for such transgressions was transfer to the Eastern Front. The dire nature of this threat not only tended to suppress any expression of decency and human kindness, it also encouraged preemptive displays of cruelty and brutality. As an organization the Wehrmacht displayed its customary obedience. It cooperated with the SS and the Einsatzgruppen and actively participated in the mass murders of Jews and others in the occupied territories of Eastern Europe.[18] When the war was lost, however, the Wehrmacht sought to place all blame for the atrocities on the SS.

Because of our isolation we were unaware of the extent of the destruction of Jewish communities. So far as we knew, the violence was a local phenomenon. We learned of the staggering extent of the killings only after being interned in the concentration camps in which our fellow inmates included Jews from all over Europe. After the war I came to realize that even the early pogroms, carried out by their Latvian henchmen, were almost certainly part of a comprehensive program orchestrated by the nazis to implement Hitler's declared policy of annihilation of the Jews.[19]

The responsibility for implementing the Final Solution in the occupied areas of the Soviet Union was assigned to the Einsatzgruppen. These mobile SS units followed the front line troops and killed all Jews (as well as gypsies and suspected communists) in the newly conquered areas. In the Baltic countries Einsatzgruppe A was active, commanded by Dr. Franz Stahlecker.[20] The chief of the Sicherheits Dienst (SD; security service—a party intelligence organization operating in parallel with the Gestapo), Reinhard Heydrich, issued a directive to use local units to do the killing. Stahlecker supervised and encouraged the activities of Latvian collaborators.[21] Working for Stahlecker was Victors Arajs, a former Latvian police officer who had become an SS officer with a rank equivalent to major. Arajs organized the Arajs Commando, a notorious group of over 200 Latvian killers, which operated as a part of Einsatzgruppe A.[22] Throughout World War II the Germans used the Arajs Commando to murder people all over Eastern Europe. In 1979 Arajs was tried by a court in Hamburg and sentenced to life imprisonment. He died in prison in 1988. The willingness of Latvians to act as hired killers is well documented. During the Bolshevik Revolution Latvian Red Raiders (Strelcii; i.e., riflemen), working for Lenin in Petrograd, were notorious executioners and killers. Latvians also were "some of the most ruthless leaders of the Cheka, Lenin's secret police, and Stalin's NKVD."[23]

From his base at the Riga Prefecture, Arajs led daily expeditions to the provinces, where the entire Jewish populations of towns and villages were rounded up and shot. All Jews living in the Latvian countryside were summarily executed in the early weeks of the German occupation. I must emphasize that although the Arajs Commando was the linchpin of these murders, Arajs received full cooperation and enthusiastic support from local Latvian officials, policemen, and volunteers.[24] The Jews had lived for generations among the local population, and many had undoubtedly established good relations and even friendships with some of the neighbors. Even so, in no reported instance were Jews protected or hidden by their Latvian neighbors. Only in Latvia's three largest cities—Riga, Daugavpils (Dvinsk), and Liepaja (Libau)—were not all Jews killed immediately. Instead they were forced into ghettos, where they found a temporary reprieve.

Our lives were increasingly controlled by a series of dehumanizing and degrading decrees. We were not permitted to walk on the sidewalks. We were no longer allowed to ride the streetcars or take horse-drawn carriages. We were forbidden to enter city parks, use playgrounds or sports fields, or visit cinemas, theaters, libraries, or museums. We were forbidden to own trucks, cars, and radios. Women could not wear hats or use umbrellas; only kerchiefs were permissible.[25] Jewish doctors and dentists were permitted to treat only Jewish patients. I had to wear a yellow star on my left breast. Soon that was deemed insufficient, and I had to wear an additional star in the middle of my back. By late August all Jews were forced to move into the ghetto. Contact with the general population was forbidden. My head was shaved. At first this applied only to men, but women were included a year or so later. In a period of less than two months my sheltered middle-class existence had come to an abrupt end. No longer considered human, I was outside the law. Nonetheless, life went on somehow.

As I mentioned before, I had read about the persecutions of Jews during the Crusades, the Spanish Inquisition, the Chmelnitzki massacres, the Kishenev pogrom. These unhappy events had occurred far away and long ago, distant from me, and, except for Kishenev, long before the twentieth century. My experience of anti-Semitism had been a few name-calling incidents, fights with kids on the street, and a few slights and insults. I was now experiencing something infinitely more threatening. The unhappy stories of the earlier pogroms and persecutions and my father's tales about the auto-da-fé, the burning at the stake of allegedly relapsed Jewish converts to Christianity during the Spanish Inquisition, had suddenly become frighteningly real. Incredibly, history had come to life, and I was afraid.

15

Riga Ghetto

⌒

The area allocated to the newly established Riga Ghetto, later called the Large Ghetto, was located in a poor, run-down suburb of Riga. Although in previous years it had been a predominantly Jewish area, it was now populated by ethnic Russians who were displaced to make room for the Jews.

Inside the designated ghetto area there were not enough housing units to accommodate the number of people forced to move there. Moreover, most of the buildings were small and dilapidated, and whole families had to squeeze into a single room. Sometimes one room was shared by several unrelated groups. Originally, 65 square feet of floor space had been allocated to each person. As space became scarce, the per-person allowance was reduced to 43 square feet.[26] Many Jews sought help finding apartments from their German employers. Officers or soldiers of individual units of the Wehrmacht and the SS came into the ghetto area and arbitrarily claimed the more desirable buildings for use by their Jewish workers.

After several trips to the ghetto area, a ninety-minute walk from our Mežaparks apartment, my father was able to find one small room, which we shared with Uncle Eduard. The second room in this apartment was occupied by another family—a couple and their teenage daughter. We all shared the kitchen. I don't know whether my father had to pay someone to get the apartment. We certainly did not pay rent once we lived in the ghetto. We moved into the ghetto in late August, taking a bare minimum of our belongings: a bed, a table and chairs, linen, clothing, dishes, pots and pans, and a few books. My father and I piled our stuff on a pushcart and negotiated the long trek to the ghetto. Most of our possessions—the furniture, carpets, piano, paintings, and other items—were simply abandoned in the city apartment, but we took some of my mother's clothing. Papa insisted: "When they took Mama away, she wore just a light summer dress. She will need her warm clothes when she comes back from prison."

Construction of a double row of barbed wire fences enclosing the designated ghetto area started soon after the order establishing the ghetto was announced. The work progressed slowly, and for some time we were able to enter and leave the ghetto area unhindered. The unfinished fence, however, was a stark reminder of the rapidly closing trap.

We expected to remain in the ghetto for a long time and believed it would offer protection from attacks by Latvian thugs. Jewish community leaders formed a committee and tried to organize essential services because the city of Riga refused to provide any services to the ghetto. Food supply and distribution, garbage disposal, sanitation, hospitals and clinics, old-age homes, and other essential services were planned and organized by the Jewish Committee under Dr. Rudolf Blumenfeld, former city physician of Riga. Supporting him were a number of prominent attorneys and civic leaders. My relative Artur Keilman headed the Social Services Department. A granduncle by marriage, he had been active in the Maccabi, a Jewish sports organization. A scrupulously honest but somewhat pretentious man, given to making momentous pronouncements, Keilman worked tirelessly trying to improve conditions in the Jewish enclave.

We felt positive about the Jewish Committee; its members were experienced and capable men, well-known and respected in the Riga Jewish community. We had confidence in them and hoped they would be successful in easing our situation and in some small measure alleviate our suffering. The committee attempted to maintain a semblance of normal life, but unfortunately the nazis had other plans.

After the war Hannah Arendt in *Eichmann in Jerusalem* accused the Jewish leadership of collaboration with the nazis:

> Wherever Jews lived, there were recognized Jewish leaders, and this leadership, almost without exception, cooperated in one way or another, for one reason or another, with the nazis. The whole truth was that if the Jewish people had been really unorganized and leaderless, there would have been chaos and plenty of misery but the total number of victims would hardly have been between four and a half and six million people.[27]

Except for isolated instances, Arendt's sweeping generalization is fundamentally untrue. It is particularly inapplicable to the situation in Latvia, where the persecution of the Jews was approved and accepted by the majority of the local population. Arendt's accusation is a calumny and a slander of the dead. It is curious that these complaints should come from Hannah Arendt, who had an ongoing relationship (starting before and renewed after World War II) with the philosopher, longtime party member, and unrepentant nazi ideologue Martin Heidegger.[28] In view of her own behavior, Arendt's accusations of collaboration by the Judenrate (Jewish councils) sound hollow, if not self-serving.

Our community leaders, decent and honorable men, believed that by dealing with the authorities they could alleviate our misery and negotiate improved conditions for the Jewish population. They followed an age-old Jewish tradition whereby prominent citizens act as go-betweens with those in power, in both the government and the church, and as spokesmen and advocates for all Jews. Like many others, these leaders fatally misjudged the nazi intentions of the Final Solution, but they did not collaborate, nor did their activities increase the number of victims. To quote Isaiah Trunk's conclusions from *Judenrat*, his definitive study of the Jewish councils in Eastern Europe: "It would appear that when all factors are considered, Jewish participation or nonparticipation in the deportations had no substantial influence—one way or another—on the final outcome of the Holocaust in Eastern Europe."[29]

Before the Riga Ghetto was closed, I worked in a nearby army warehouse where war booty captured from the Red Army was collected and sorted. Boots, coats, underwear, and other supply items were plentiful, but we had no access to weapons or ammunition. Our Jewish contingent included men from different backgrounds: professionals, artisans, and members of the working class. I was one of the youngest. It was here that I first met Samuel (Mulya) Atlas. He took me under his wing and, although eighteen years my senior, treated me as an equal. Mulya had many acquaintances among our coworkers, who followed his example, and I was accepted as a member of a close circle of friends. I was proud of his friendship and am still grateful for it. Mulya and I renewed our friendship about a year later when we again met at a different workplace. We stayed together during all our time in the concentration camps, and I found in him a steady support, a veritable tower of strength.

Our work at the warehouse ended soon after the ghetto was closed. We received no pay for working on this or any of our other assignments. Our employers contracted with the German authorities for the use of our labor. The Germans established a Ghetto Labor Office, which supplied both skilled and unskilled Jewish workers to German armed forces units and to private firms and which collected wages from our employers.

Two incidents from my work assignments during the early days of the nazi occupation remain etched in my mind. While cleaning one of the apartments requisitioned by the German army, I was told to fix a stuffed, overflowing toilet. I had no tools, not even gloves; nor did I know how a commode worked. It was a revolting task, but I started to empty the overflowing fixture. Fortunately, by removing the stuffed-up material with my bare hands, I was able to restore the toilet to working order. It was a task that needed to be done rather than a phony one deliberately contrived to degrade me, and I did not feel abused; still, it left me with an intimation of worse things to come.

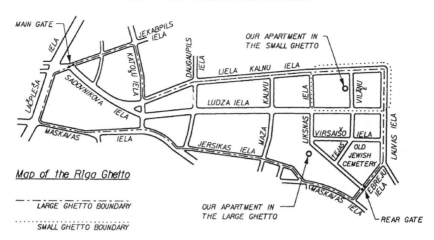

Map of Riga Ghetto.

A second upsetting experience happened several weeks later. One afternoon in late September, a fellow worker and I were sent to a nearby hospital to bury a patient who had recently died. We were accompanied by a German soldier because Jews were no longer permitted to walk unescorted in the city. We found a pushcart and picked up the body, wrapped in sheets, at the hospital. The dead man was a Russian, but I could not tell whether he was a civilian or a soldier. We were ordered to take him to a Russian Orthodox cemetery several blocks away. Hauling the bouncing cart through the cobblestone streets, we had to hold on to the body to prevent it from falling off the cart. Finally, we reached the cemetery. A caretaker showed us where to dig, and we went to work. It was late afternoon, and we were anxious to get back to the ghetto, but the caretaker insisted on a 6-foot-deep grave. As we lowered the body into it, I wondered, who was this man? Did he have any loved ones? Was someone waiting for him to return? It was my first direct encounter with death, and it seemed very undignified. Nobody said any prayers, and nobody mourned at this unceremonious ending of a man's life. We quickly filled in the grave and hurried away in the growing darkness. As undignified as the burial may have seemed to me at the time, it was a harbinger of things to come. Although there was no casket, the body, wrapped in a shroud, was carefully lowered into the individual grave. It was a decent burial when viewed from the perspective of the events that occurred just two months later. Then the bodies of victims were dumped helter-skelter into mass graves.

I had taken a number of books with me into the ghetto, and I spent much of my evenings and weekends reading. Among the books I read was Franz Werfel's *The Forty Days of the Musa Dagh,* a fictionalized account of the 1915 Armenian genocide by the Turkish government. Werfel's dramatic tale of the appalling atrocities made an indelible impression. The Turkish government was determined to eradicate the entire Armenian community. The genocide involved forced deportations: the Armenian population was marched into the desert under inhuman conditions, without food or water, and with inconceivable gratuitous brutality. Men, women, and children were killed indiscriminately. I was struck by the similarity between events described in the book and our own situation. Although the book also gave a clear indication of things to come, I did not appreciate it at the time. For me it was a disturbing account of the oppression of a defenseless minority, an object lesson of man's inhumanity to man.

Werfel describes the armed resistance of a small group of Armenians in a mountain stronghold. The survivors of this fight are rescued by warships of the allied navies. For the majority of Armenians, however, there was no effective intervention and no rescue. That, too, was a realistic preview of what help we could expect from the outside world. A German clergyman had tried unsuccessfully to intercede for his fellow Christians. The German government, however, did not want to strain relations with its World War I ally, Turkey, and did nothing to support the clergyman's efforts.

Expecting a long stay in the ghetto, I was concerned about my education. As formal schooling was not going to be available, I attempted to study trigonometry on my own and arranged to take lessons from Peter's former mathematics teacher. Unfortunately, events in the ghetto abruptly terminated this project after just three lessons.

Enclosed by double rows of barbed wire fence and ringed by Latvian SS guards, the Riga Ghetto was sealed off on October 25, 1941. The gates were shut, and free entry and exit were barred. We were permitted out only for work assignments, marching in columns with a gentile escort. The sidewalks along the fence were off limits, and all traffic within the ghetto moved through the backyards and interior streets. Anyone appearing at the fence was shot on sight by the Latvian guards. The ghetto became an isolated universe, light-years removed from the life of the city. Workers returning from the city were frequently searched at the ghetto gate. Anyone caught with food or other articles was shot on the spot or taken to prison to be killed later.

After the ghetto was closed, our living conditions deteriorated rapidly. Sanitation was a serious problem, and maintaining cleanliness was difficult. Our rations were half those given to the general population, and even these were often undelivered and unavailable. Many families had caches of hoarded staples: cereals, rice, sugar, salt, potatoes, a few canned goods. We tried to protect these precious supplies, preserving them for a future time when real starvation was upon us.

In our apartment the three of us—my father, Uncle Eduard, and I—living in one small room still had some semblance of privacy. A realization of just how terrible conditions in the ghetto were first became evident to me when I visited my grandaunt Rosalya Lazarevna Hirschfeld in the newly established ghetto old-age home. Before the war she had lived near us in one of our family-owned apartment buildings around the corner from the factory. Although not disabled and only in her early sixties, she had been unable to find a place of her own in the ghetto and had to move into the old-age home. Rosalya Lazarevna had lost her husband during World War I, and her only son, Kolya (Nikolai), had died fifteen years earlier from typhoid fever at age twenty-three. An unhappy and difficult woman, she had eked out a living making children's games. Rosalya Lazarevna had spent a good deal of time with me when I was younger. She had very strong feelings about Tchaikovsky and about his relationship with his patron, Nadejda von Meck. She repeatedly told me about the composer and was vehement in her indignation. "Imagine, such a cad," she would exclaim. "He would take money from her but would never even consent to meet her."

I liked Rosalya Lazarevna and felt obligated to visit. I had never been to an old-age home. The home consisted of one large hall with beds jammed side by side along both long walls. There were no screens or partitions—no privacy at all. The room was poorly ventilated; the air was stale and oppressive. I found our conversation difficult and depressing. After spending just a short time with her, I felt suffocated and made my escape.

In November members of the Latvian nazi party, the Perkonkrusts, suddenly burst into our apartment in the Large Ghetto and arrested Uncle Eduard. He was held at their headquarters but was released after one week. I do not know why he was arrested. Perkonkrusts was notorious for its "interrogations" (a euphemism for torture), however, and I was aware that Eduard had been tortured. He was rearrested just prior to the liquidation of the Large Ghetto in late November, and we never saw or heard from him again.

Eduard may have been questioned because of his contacts with Latvians or perhaps because of his activities in socialist or labor organizations. He may have been denounced by someone bearing a grudge. About two years later, while in the Little Ghetto and working in the city, I talked briefly with my grandmother's former nurse, Paulina Streipa, a Latvian. She had contacted me, and we arranged to meet at my place of work. Paulina wanted to know what had happened to Uncle Eduard. It seems that at about the time of his arrest she, too, had been questioned. She did not tell me who questioned her or what they had wanted to know. Our meeting was brief; Paulina

16

Aktion:
The Destruction of the Riga Ghetto

In mid-November 1941 vague rumors began to circulate: our ghetto would be closed, and we would be resettled in some work camp farther east. Within a few days workmen started to erect a barbed wire fence, partitioning off a two-block area in the far corner of the ghetto. This section was to become a barracks camp for men of working age, while all other residents of the Riga Ghetto were to be evacuated to an undisclosed destination. The prospect of being sent away from Riga was very unsettling. However bad the conditions might be, in Riga one at least had some knowledge of the local area and language. There was no reason to believe we would be better off somewhere else. In fact, it was a fair guess that it would be even worse.

Adding to my apprehension was the realization that no one seemed to know what was going on. The surviving leaders of the Jewish community, our rabbis, doctors, and attorneys, could offer no suggestions about what to do. Nor were any of those to whom I customarily looked for guidance of any help. My father, teachers, relatives—not one of them had any better insights than I. In the face of this uncertainty, the tension in the ghetto mounted almost hourly. It was clear that something was going to happen.

The liquidation began late Saturday night, November 29, 1941. Swarms of drunken German and uniformed Latvian SS troops, armed with rifles, descended on the western half of the ghetto. They broke into the houses and drove the startled residents into the streets. So sudden was the onslaught that half-cooked dishes were left on stoves, and meals remained uneaten. The attackers were in a drunken frenzy, kicking and clubbing those who did not move fast enough to suit them. Children were torn from their mothers' arms and hurled out of windows. It was only because our house was located in the eastern part of the Riga Ghetto, an area not subject to evacuation that day, that I was not forced out that weekend.

The next day, Sunday, I was up early. It was just beginning to get light on a cold, gray wintry morning. I cautiously ventured out into the yard to see what was happening. Our yard faced Liksnas iela and was separated from the street by a wooden fence. Through a crack in the half-closed gate I could look down toward the corner of Ludzas iela, the central street of the ghetto. At that moment a column of my fellow Jews had just turned the corner onto our street, which led to the rear exit of the ghetto. They marched in complete silence, five abreast, flanked by a phalanx of uniformed German and Latvian SS guards with bayonets fixed. During the preceding week I had been in a state of high anxiety and experienced repeated panic attacks. The sight of the approaching column filled me with a sense of imminent doom. Not waiting for the column to pass my hiding place, I dashed back to the safety of our house.

With typical German punctuality, at exactly 1 P.M. an SS commander came into the ghetto and announced that the *Aktion* (action), the nazi euphemism for organized killings, was over, and we were again permitted out into the streets. I immediately dragged Papa into the so-called work camp in the corner of the Large Ghetto, which had recently been fenced off and established as a camp for men of working age. It offered the relative safety of remaining in Riga, a temporary reprieve from deportation to the unknown. Women were not permitted to cross into the camp, and separation from wives and children kept many husbands and fathers from seeking the protection of the work camp.

In the work camp (henceforth referred to by its common name, the Little Ghetto) my father and I quickly found a place to stay, joining a group of acquaintances in a tiny one-room apartment. As soon as we were settled, I went back to the entrance of the Little Ghetto in the hope of learning more about the fate of the deportees. Later that afternoon Jewish ghetto police grabbed me, along with a number of other men, for a burial detail. The Old Jewish Cemetery was located in a nearby corner of the Large Ghetto. We were led there under police escort and told to dig a large grave. During the evacuation many people had been killed inside the ghetto. While we were digging the grave, other groups carted the dead to the cemetery and dumped the bodies on the old graves. The cemetery was full, and we dug right on top of existing graves. The ground was frozen, and having to chop through the soil with pickaxes was difficult and tedious work. Once through the frozen ground we found gravelly sand, and the digging went faster. Five or 6 feet down we uncovered the bones of the previous occupants of the graves. I tried to dislodge the old bones with my shovel and was severely rebuked by one of the older men in our group. Jewish law forbids disturbing the dead.

Another controversy arose when we started to lower the dead into the grave. Our orthodox coworkers insisted that according to Jewish law, men

One of the mass graves at Rumbuli, Riga, 1993.

and women cannot be buried in the same grave. The younger men objected; it meant having to dig another grave. I asked what they thought would happen—indiscretions between the sexes? In the end, however, we did dig a separate grave. That afternoon I helped bury about 100 people. Somebody quietly said *El Male Rachamim* and Kaddish (the prayers for the dead). My most vivid memory is seeing the body of an infant girl sprawled across the mound of one of the old graves. There were no signs of injury, no blood: she looked just like a broken doll.

Although it would seem to have been difficult to avoid the realization that sooner or later (and probably sooner) I, too, was going to be killed, I still managed to deny it. I distanced myself from the victims. They must have brought this catastrophe upon themselves. They must have done something forbidden. Perhaps they had resisted the evacuation or tried to hide, or they were too old, too young, or too weak to march in the columns. Could I, by avoiding their mistakes, ensure my survival?

In the days that followed, rumors of killings reached the ghetto. The stories claimed that instead of being resettled, our relatives and friends were marched to a nearby forest where they all were killed. A young woman claimed to have witnessed the massacre. According to her, the killings had taken place in Rumbuli Forest, about 7 miles away. After being forced to strip naked, the evacuees had been machine-gunned and dumped into prepared mass graves. She and one other woman had avoided this fate by hiding under the heap of discarded shoes. She managed to crawl out under cover of darkness and to make her way back to the ghetto. But we were as yet unprepared to admit the truth. We said she had lost her mind. The truth was just too terrifying. Instead we clung to reports that our women and children had been sighted in a camp near Salaspils, a short distance beyond the Rumbuli killing site. Contributing to the confusion was the fact that women and children had indeed been seen there. But as we later realized, they were Jews who had recently arrived in transports from Germany.

Many people, including myself, desperately tried to hear and believe any good news. We became angry when fellow inmates said our loved ones had been killed. We summarily dismissed such people as pessimists. As time went on, however, there were fewer and fewer encouraging rumors, and nobody heard any good news. Slowly, most of us began to accept what until then had been unthinkable. I again thought of this massacre as yet another isolated, local atrocity, not the implementation of the nazis' Final Solution of killing all Jews.

The week following the first *Aktion* was a period of unreality, of suspended animation. Whatever the truth about the events of the previous weekend and the fate of our relatives and friends, the precariousness of our situation was painfully clear. We lived in anticipation of impending disaster, waiting from day to day for another blow to fall.

An eyewitness report of the aftermath of the first *Aktion* is given by Abraham Shpungin:

> Now the Germans spread rumors, that no more people would be evacuated; whoever has remained in the ghetto will stay there. It was done to calm the population remaining in the eastern half of the ghetto. People even related that through Latvian acquaintances some relatives in the ghetto had received letters from their kin evacuated in the first *Aktion*. The kin supposedly wrote that they are now in camps not far from Riga, that they don't lack anything, that they are all well and healthy. It was said that people had even seen such letters. It is evident that these were forgeries. Or else people had been forced to write them prior to being shot. However incredible it was, people wanted to believe it, if only to feel comforted and reassured. They grasped for it as a drowning man grasps for a straw. Many men who already were in the Little Ghetto, the men's camp, did now in deadly danger steal through the fence back to their families in the Large Ghetto.[30]

During the week that followed the first *Aktion* I worked in the city every day. On Saturday we were permitted to cross over into the Large Ghetto. I took that opportunity to visit my friend and classmate Lyuba Treskunoff and also my cousin Ella Hirschfeld Asarch. My meeting with Lyuba was very painful. Our conversation, usually free and animated, was forced and difficult. To what camp would she be sent? When and where would we meet again? I felt a terrible sadness and guilt for not being able to do anything to help her. Later, after the subsequent events had unfolded, I found myself thinking that there must have been something I could have done. Should I have tried to smuggle her into the Little Ghetto? Could I have saved her? I have never been able to satisfy myself on this score. However irrational, I still have a lingering sense of having failed.

Ella, the daughter of one of Grandmother Emma's brothers, a widow with no children, had frequently visited our home. She had taken great interest in me, and I had been a frequent visitor to her apartment. Now I found her in a tiny room in one of

Lyuba Treskunoff, 1939.

the few multistory buildings of the ghetto. The room had barely enough space to accommodate the bed; there were no table or chairs. This visit was not as painful as the one with Lyuba. Ella seemed in a relatively good mood. We sat on the bed and chatted.

The liquidation of the eastern half of the Large Ghetto resumed later that weekend. It followed the pattern of the earlier killings. On Sunday night, December 7, drunken hordes of SS again descended on the ghetto. The people were thrust out onto the streets and, after long delays, were marched off to Rumbuli. Once there, they were forced to strip naked and were machine-gunned into waiting mass graves. The massacre continued into Monday, December 8, 1941.

The liquidation of the Riga Ghetto was planned and directed by SS General Friedrich Jeckeln, Higher SS and Police Leader North, a unit attached to the Einsatzgruppen.[31] He had recently taken over the command in this area. Eager to demonstrate his skill at solving the Jewish problem, he organized a surprise attack against the local Jews. A frequent, sinister presence in the ghetto, Obersturmführer (lieutenant) Dr. Rudolf Lange, later Sturmbannführer (major), commander of Einsatzkommando 2c, led the assault.[32] Victors Arajs, the notorious head of the Arajs Commando, had a major role in the killings, as did another popular Latvian hero, the decorated flyer and army officer Herberts Cukurs. The latter's reputation for brutality and viciousness was such that he became known as the "butcher of Riga." Dr. M. Weinreich, who ran the infirmary in the Liepaja (Libau) Ghetto, was an eyewitness to Cukurs's unimaginable sadism. One day Cukurs came to the infirmary in search of hidden, work-capable men and women. Storming into the women's section, he discovered a newborn baby. Births in the ghetto were forbidden. Cukurs tore the baby from its mother's bed, dashed its head against the wall, and dropped the lifeless body on the floor.[33] In 1965 Cukurs's corpse was found in a trunk at a beach house in Montevideo. After the war he and many other nazi war criminals had sought refuge in South America. Cukurs, who lived in São Paulo, was lured to Montevideo and executed by a group calling itself Those Who Shall Never Forget. According to a report in the *New York Times,* the group announced the execution in West Germany and disclosed where the body could be found.[34]

In 1946 Jeckeln and six other nazi generals were tried and hanged by the Soviets in Riga. At his trial Jeckeln stated: "The number of Jews brought to Latvia from abroad is unknown to me, as is the number of Jews killed in Latvia. Even before the German takeover, so many Jews were exterminated by the Latvians that no exact count could be established." Asked why Jews had been brought to Latvia for destruction, he stated, "Latvia provided a suitable soil (*einen geeigneten Boden*) for these murders."[35]

The victims of the Large *Aktion* included:

Zhenya Kaplan Kretzer (mother of my cousin Ali),
her daughter, my cousin Miriam (Mia),
and Charlotte (Lotte) Kretzer Kaplan;
my great-aunt Ella Saltzman Michelson (mother of my cousin
   Mako),
her daughter Emma,
her son Siegfried (Fredi) Michelson,
his wife, Slova Meilach Michelson,
their son Samuel,
her sister-in-law Ella Michelson Dawidson (mother of Paul
   Dawidson);
Zhenya Gruenstein Kretzer (wife of Dr. Viktor Kretzer),
her daughter Noemi and son David;
my great-aunt Rosalya Lazarevna Hirschfeld;
my cousins Ella Hirschfeld Asarch and Klara Hirschfeld Friedberg;
Lilly Michelson Keilman (wife of Artur Keilman),
her daughter Emma;
our family friend Rosa Lurie.

Among my friends and classmates killed were:

Harriet Grossman,
Vitaly (Talik) Levontin,
Helga and Sylvia Lippert,
Mischa Lippert,
Mischa Schatz,
Boris Schmulowich,
Lyuba Treskunoff,
her parents and sister Esya,
and many, many others.

17
ℒittle 𝒢hetto

𝒻ive months after the nazis had taken over ℛiga, our entire Jewish community was gone. The majority of my relatives and friends were killed during the liquidation of the ghetto, which we later called the *Large Aktion*. Just thirty-seven days after being locked in the Large Ghetto, most of us—about 27,000 people—had been killed. In the Little Ghetto, the barbed wire–enclosed enclave in the corner of the former ghetto, about 4,500 people remained, among them just 500 women and only 20 to 30 children. Many of the women were seamstresses who had worked for the Germans. During the *Aktion* they had been taken to prison and later brought to the Little Ghetto. The Little Ghetto was not a safe haven, it was just another way station on the road to total annihilation.

My father and I were among about 4,000 men crowded into the Little Ghetto. Our living conditions had been poor in the Large Ghetto. Now they were worse. The buildings in the Little Ghetto were older, smaller, and more dilapidated. In the Large Ghetto there had been a space allocation of 43 square feet per person. Here there was no allocation; as many people as possible squeezed into any available space. An apartment like ours, consisting of one small room and a tiny kitchen and intended to house a single individual or a small family, was now home to around ten men. In our rush to escape the Large Ghetto, we had left behind what few possessions we had; we had literally taken just the clothes on our backs. We hung what little clothing we had on a nail above our mattress. At night we covered the entire floor with mattresses, all side by side. Still, our circumstances were almost luxurious—given what was to come. We each had our own mattress. In the concentration camps, where three of us had to share a single straw pallet, we could only dream of such an extravagance. We were not subject to constant surveillance by our jailers and enjoyed a modicum of privacy in spite of the crowded conditions. We could look forward to spending evenings and weekends in our apartment in the company of friends.

The Little Ghetto was a work camp. Life became a mechanical routine. Day in, day out, hot or cold, rain or shine, snow or sleet, we trudged into town to work and back home again to the ghetto, always escorted by a gentile. Our jobs included janitorial and maintenance tasks. We chopped and carried wood for the brick ovens that heated many city apartments. We moved looted furniture into apartments being prepared for the German occupiers. The few surviving Jewish women—our mothers, wives, daughters, and sisters—became cleaning women. Jewish artisans worked in their various crafts: tailors, shoemakers, glove makers, carpenters, and locksmiths. Some of us became instant apprentices. There were also jobs in lumber mills, on earth-moving projects, in peat bogs and other godforsaken places. Good jobs were indoors, especially where food could be found or where something could be stolen and traded for food. But taking items back into the ghetto was extremely hazardous. The SS would occasionally frisk the returning columns and summarily execute anyone caught with food or any other item. Boots, always in demand, could be smuggled into the ghetto with little risk. You went to work wearing old, ready-to-be-discarded boots and exchanged them for good ones, which could be sold or traded in the ghetto.

My father became very depressed. Going into the Little Ghetto he made no mention of bringing my mother's warm winter clothing. He must have realized that my mother was dead, but he never talked about it. Unable to face the daily trek into town, he found some work inside the Little Ghetto. On Bloody Tuesday, December 9, 1941, the day after the second, eastern half of the Large Ghetto was emptied during the so-called Second *Aktion,* Latvian police units combed the now vacant ghetto for hideouts. Those found were shot on the spot or taken to the nearby Bikernieku Forest and killed there. The Little Ghetto was also emptied, and all who had remained there were rounded up. Loaded into blue city buses, they, too, were taken to the Bikernieku Forest, where they were murdered.

When I returned from work that evening, Papa was not in our apartment as he had been on previous nights. He did not come back the next evening or on any of those that followed. Slowly I began to understand what had happened. I did not grieve; I was numb. I had seen people killed, I had buried some of those killed in the Large Ghetto; it was obvious what lay in store for us all. My parents had disappeared. Nobody saw or reported them killed; there was no burial, no closure. Although it seemed likely that they were both dead, it was as if they had just left. At first I did not admit to myself that they had been killed. Slowly, over the next years in the camps, the overwhelming evidence of the wholesale killings convinced me that they were dead. Even so, only years later, long after my liberation, did I say Kaddish for them.

In the Little Ghetto just a few of my relatives remained: my granduncle Artur Keilman and his son David (Dadi), who was a member of the Jewish ghetto police. Artur Keilman, together with Max Wand, a German Jewish refugee, were the Jewish leaders in charge of the Little Ghetto. My cousins Max (Mako) Michelson and Paul Dawidson were my only other close relatives. Working at the clinic was our family friend and distant relative Dr. Viktor (Vitya) Kretzer. When he lost his wife and two young children in the liquidation of the Large Ghetto, Dr. Kretzer had tried to commit suicide but was saved by his colleagues. He later died in the camps in Germany. In charge of the clinic and infirmary of the Little Ghetto was Professor Vladimir Mintz, the famous Riga surgeon who had treated Lenin. Some months later I benefited from his surgical skills. I had injured my hand while chopping wood at work. After returning to the ghetto I went to the infirmary, where Professor Mintz closed the gaping wound using small metal clamps instead of sutures. Fortunately, I had not hit the bone, there was no infection, and my hand healed rapidly.

On weekends, a group of my roommates played bridge. I loved watching the game and listened eagerly to their banter, but no one offered to teach me the game. Sundays we did not work, and I spent a good deal of time with my cousin Paul Dawidson, a gentle man in his mid-thirties with a great sense of humor. We became very close, and I grew to love him. He told me about his prewar life as a clothing salesman in a fashionable menswear store. Life before the war was a topic dear to us all. I was fascinated listening to tales recounted by my older coworkers and roommates—tales about expensive restaurants and gourmet food, about their businesses and travels, and occasionally intimate anecdotes about their lovers. But the men never talked about their children. Weekends and evenings I also visited with my few remaining friends. Our circle of friends had shrunk significantly, but now, because of the shared horrors, friendships seemed more intense. I had given up all thoughts of continuing my studies, but I still read a lot. Books in our room were considered common property, and I had a considerable variety of titles from which to choose.

One of the men who shared our apartment in the Little Ghetto was Victor (Vitya) Kron. He was the younger son of Dr. Isidore Kron, a longtime friend of our family and my grandmother's attending physician. I believe we were distantly related. Victor Kron was thirty years old, a forthright and forceful man. Unmarried and with natural leadership qualities, he was one of the notable personalities in our apartment. He was probably in one of the professions. He was well educated, well-spoken, and had an incisive sense of humor, which he used effectively in conversations. After my father's disappearance, Herr Kron (as I always addressed him) suggested that we pool our resources and support each other. A person with high ethical standards, his only condition for sharing our life and our provisions was no stealing. He explained his personal moral code: "An honest person does not steal. Stealing is always wrong, regardless from whom or under what circumstances. I do not steal, not even from the nazis." Herr Kron and I worked at the same place. When I showed some interest in a co-worker, a German Jewish girl, I quickly learned there was another condition for our cooperation: no chasing skirts. Herr Kron became a substitute parent, correcting and chastising me as he saw fit. Although grateful for his interest in me, I was in awe of him. Herr Kron was always correct but also a little stiff. I did not find him a warm person, and he did not inspire me to confide in him.

Kron had a gentile sister-in-law who lived in the city and with whom he remained in contact. Working for the Germans in apartment buildings in the city made it easy to arrange meetings with gentiles in basements or backyards. Through her he bartered valuables and jewelry received from his fellow ghetto inmates for items of food that, in spite of the danger, he would bring back into the ghetto. A few months later, in June 1942, he was caught at the gate with a loaf of bread and some money. Kron was summarily hanged by the nazi commandant.

For me, the sudden disruption of a newly established relationship was devastating. During the difficult days after my father's disappearance, Kron had been a rock of strength and a stabilizing influence. I valued his good judgment and admired his unwavering sense of right and wrong. He provided guidance and support, and I relied on him for day-to-day advice and encouragement. Just as I had begun to know and feel closer to him, Herr Kron was killed. Our relationship never had a chance to develop into a warm friendship. His death occurred a few short months after my father's disappearance, and this time I could not deny what had happened. I continued to live in the same apartment, but I was now very much on my own. I was not close to any of my other roommates.

The daily routine of the Little Ghetto was frequently interrupted by beatings, searches, selections, or killings. Jews were outside the law. The penalty for any offense, real or imagined, was death. Death remained a constant presence throughout my years in the camps. It hovered over us, striking capriciously out of the blue. Possessing a loaf of bread or a banknote, being in the wrong place at the wrong time, having the wrong facial expression—anything at all—became a pretext for killing Jews. The fact was that no reason was needed. Literally, a step out of line could provoke a murderous attack. I tried to avoid being noticed, avoid eye contact, make myself invisible. At work I learned to walk purposefully, always carrying some tool—a hammer, screwdriver, or wrench—to give the impression that I was on a legitimate errand.

Even the random nature of much of the violence was calculated. The very pointlessness of the killings and the brutality that characterized them were meant to instill terror. The Germans and their Latvian henchmen enjoyed toying with their victims. It was a sadist's wildest dream come true. The murderers loved their work.

Having witnessed the killings during the evacuation of the ghetto and seeing the continuing violence in the Little Ghetto, I could no longer deny how precarious our situation was. I did, however, try to lessen the threat of imminent death that was staring me in the face. I tried to maintain some control of my own fate. I wanted to discover what the victims had done to precipitate the fatal attack. What moves and actions should I avoid? In truth, the nazis never needed a pretext to kill us. People were killed through no fault of their own—avoiding death became in large part a matter of luck.

The Reichsjuden Ghetto – German Jews in Riga

After the liquidation of its Latvian Jewish inmates, a part of the Large Ghetto was used to settle Jews deported from Germany. Latvian Jews believed the nazis gave preferential treatment to the Jews now being expelled from Germany and that our families had been killed to make housing available for them. We were not alone in this belief. Jeanette Wolff, a German Jewish survivor of the Riga Ghetto, expressed a similar opinion in her memoirs.[36] Even as Latvian Jews tried to help the new arrivals with food and advice, they resented their presence. In fact, not all arrivals from Germany came to the ghetto, now called the Reichsjuden Ghetto (the ghetto of Jews from the German Reich). Jews arriving from Germany on other transports were taken directly to the nearby forests and killed. Those brought to the ghetto were predominantly women, children, and older men. The younger men from these transports had been separated from their families and sent to nearby camps like Salaspils, where most were killed or starved to death under unbelievably brutal conditions. At first we knew nothing of all this, and the bad feelings persisted for a long time. Only after it became painfully clear that the nazis murdered Jews indiscriminately did we begin to see the German Jews as fellow victims.

In retrospect, I am ashamed of denying our shared ethnicity. At the time we thought of the German Jews as more German than Jewish. Gertrude Schneider related that although Jews could have left Germany between 1933 and 1939, "evidently they had felt so secure, so 'German,' that many of them considered leaving their country unthinkable."[37] Among the deportees to Riga were decorated veterans of World War I, proud of their contributions to the German Reich. There also were converts to Catholicism, who continued to celebrate mass in the ghetto. Many German Jews disliked the Ostjuden (Eastern European Jews), and we reciprocated the feeling.

Among the Latvian Jews, especially those from Courland, many had been strongly influenced by German culture. This included my family and most of our relatives. Germany was not our country, however, and we never thought of ourselves as Germans. An anecdote, actually considered amusing, was repeatedly told in my family. One summer an old Jewish beggar approached Peter and me as we were playing in the front yard of our villa at Jurmala. "Do Jews live here?" he asked. I answered directly, "Oh no, my cousin is German, and I am Latvian." The poor man fled. I must have been four years old.

The Little Ghetto for the Latvian Jews and the Reichsjuden Ghetto were physically independent entities located on opposite sides of the common central street, Ludzas iela. From this street separate gates led into the two ghettos, and we were permitted access only to our respective ghettos. The German Jews renamed the streets in their ghetto, replacing the unfamiliar Latvian names with German ones reflecting the places of origin of the various transports. Men from our Little Ghetto courted the newly arrived women from Germany. The German Jews had a more casual and open attitude toward sex than the local Jewish population, among whom Victorian mores still prevailed. Communicating was easy, as most Latvian Jews spoke good German. With the tacit approval of the ghetto commandant, passes permitting visits to the German Ghetto were readily obtained from our Latvian Jewish ghetto police. Lasting friendships developed; some resulted in so-called ghetto marriages, later formalized by the few couples lucky enough to survive. The Latvian Jews had better contacts in the city and were able to provide food and other necessities to the German Jews, who found themselves at a disadvantage in a strange and hostile environment. A pound of butter would buy sexual favors. I recall how our roommate Davidoff, a pharmacist, would groom and anoint himself prior to his weekend forays into the German Ghetto. We disliked him and made merciless fun of him and his meticulous preliminary ablutions. In the Little Ghetto this fraternization provoked considerable controversy. The older men felt that by consorting with the German Jews we were being disloyal to our murdered kin, but the younger men were not deterred.

The daily routine of life in the Reichsjuden Ghetto, like that in the Little Ghetto, unfolded against a background of continuous disruption and violence. It is heartbreaking to read the memoirs and descriptions of life in the Reichsjuden Ghetto. Searches, arrests, killings were the order of the day. The violence was vicious and sadistic, such as children being murdered in the presence of their mothers and vice versa. The sadism was particularly repulsive because it was frequently targeted at little children. Our nazi jailers committed atrocities so inhuman that I, too, would be skeptical had I not witnessed such incidents, which convinced me never to underestimate the nazis' (or, for that matter, man's) propensity and appetite for wanton cruelty.

OUR JAILERS

The Germans with whom we had the most contact could roughly be separated into two groups: those whose responsibilities led them to view the

Jews as an exploitable labor resource and the murderers. The former group wanted the Jews to work efficiently and to get as much work done as possible. To that end they generally tried to maintain reasonable conditions for the Jews under their supervision and, to some limited extent, protect them from gratuitous harassment by the SS. Our German employers occasionally tried to intercede with the SS ghetto authorities to protect their Jewish workers from being taken away and killed. They insisted that they must have their Jews, that these workers were indispensable. Sometimes our employers prevailed, but it was nevertheless only a temporary reprieve.

The latter group, the killers, included the SS and the Gestapo, represented in Riga by the above-mentioned Dr. Rudolf Lange; Obersturmführer (lieutenant) Kurt Krause, the commandant of the ghetto; and his successor, Obersturmführer Eduard Roschmann, all notable sadists. Summary executions occurred almost daily. During the initial weeks of the German occupation, the Latvians had appeared to be particularly bloodthirsty and committed most of the atrocities. Now the murders were also committed by the Germans. Lange was the highest-ranking SS officer frequently seen in the ghetto and the most feared. We knew him by sight. Whenever he appeared it meant trouble, and we desperately tried to disappear. Wherever Jews were being killed, Lange was there. As often as not, he did the killing himself.

Ghetto commander Krause and his lieutenants participated in acts of wanton violence and killings. Krause was Viennese, and he developed a tenuous rapport with some of the German Jews deported to Riga from that city. That, however, did not deter him from committing acts of extreme cruelty and sadism. An impulsive and unpredictable sadist, he could be excessively cordial and solicitous at one moment and become a frenzied killer in the next. On several occasions he killed children in front of their parents and parents in front of their children. Krause's instant reaction to any infraction was to pull his revolver and kill.[38]

When Krause was replaced by Roschmann in early 1943, we were happy finally to be rid of this madman. Roschmann, a lawyer, was indeed more deliberate, less likely to react by killing his victims on the spur of the moment. Roschmann, however, was a careful and meticulous investigator who would incarcerate and interrogate suspects and implicate and arrest many more people than Krause had. As a result, our situation did not improve, and the number of people killed under Roschmann was even larger than that under Krause.

Resistance – Weapons in the Ghetto

On October 28, 1942, a truck carrying eleven young Jewish men from the Little Ghetto was stopped by the Gestapo on the highway out of Riga. The men had recruited a Latvian driver to take them in the direction of Daugavpils (Dvinsk), where they planned to join the partisans. In the ensuing shoot-out the Jews threw hand grenades, instantly killing three of the

Gestapo. All but two of the Jews died in the shoot-out, and the survivors, one critically wounded, managed to get back to the ghetto. The wounded man died a short time later, and the other survivor was later captured and executed. We surmised at the time that the escape was a Gestapo provocation; the Latvian driver was seen leaving the scene together with the fourth, lightly wounded Gestapo man. Our suspicions were confirmed after the war. Documents found in the German archives showed that the Gestapo had requested a loan of army license plates for the truck that was to carry the escapees; using Gestapo plates would have aroused suspicion.

Early the following Saturday, October 31, there was great excitement in the Little Ghetto. While our work commandos mustered on Vilanu Street, SS troops armed with rifles swarmed through the ghetto. As the commandos left the ghetto, the ghetto commandant and his assistants dragged a number of people, most of them elderly, from the ranks of the departing columns. That morning the SS also ordered the Latvian Jewish Police to march to a roll call on the Blechplatz (Tin Square) in the Reichsjuden Ghetto. It was assumed to be a postponed routine police assembly, normally held every Friday. As the police column approached the square, they sensed trouble and became uneasy. Their leader, Anatoli Nathan, called out for them to run and try to save themselves. The SS opened fire from concealed machine guns, killing thirty-nine of our policemen on the spot. Among the victims was my cousin David Keilman.

While at work in the Riga Dairy located near the ghetto, I could hear the shooting. It was a lovely, warm fall day. I remember thinking how incongruous it was that the sun would be shining so brightly on the appalling events in the ghetto. The murder of our ghetto police was a terrible blow. All of them were well-known to us. They were our relatives and friends, and we liked and trusted them. They had frequently been helpful and had always tried to protect us to the best of their ability. In short, they were family. Including the hostages, who had been plucked from the departing columns, 150 men were killed in reprisal for the 3 slain Gestapo.

Two Jewish policemen, Meilach Damsky and Sascha Israelowitz, were able to slip away and hide during the massacre and then disappear. When Damsky was apprehended some months later in a hideout in the ghetto, Commandant Krause killed him on the spot. Israelowitz managed to leave the ghetto with one of the work commandos. He remained in hiding for several months in town, first with friends at a Jewish workshop operated by and for the Gestapo and later with two Christian women. He was ultimately betrayed to the Gestapo and fell into the hands of Roschmann. Rather than execute Israelowitz on the spot, Roschmann arrested him and subjected him to a lengthy interrogation in Riga Central Prison.

Unrelated to the attempted escape and prior to the reprisal killings of the Latvian Jewish ghetto police, a number of our men had organized a resistance movement in the Little Ghetto.[39] After the loss of their families, many men were certain the nazis were determined to kill us all. The men were in a desperate mood, and the murder of our police confirmed that belief. Even though defeat and death would be the inevitable result of an uprising, they were determined to resist the nazi oppressors and, if necessary, to die fighting.

The movement was led by Owsey Okun, who had been part-owner of a textile factory in Dvinsk, and attorney Jakob Jewelson, former administrator of the finance department of the Jewish Committee in the Large Ghetto. They were assisted by Yitzhak Bag, a senior member of the Latvian Jewish ghetto police. Many younger men from the Little Ghetto, as well as some members of the Latvian Jewish ghetto police, were involved in the resistance movement. The group built hideouts and started to stockpile weapons and supplies in the ghetto in preparation for a future revolt against the nazis. At several places of work in the city, including the work commando Pulverturm, Jews sorted, cleaned, and preserved captured military equipment. The weapons were unaccounted for and could easily be removed and disposed of without danger of discovery. Weapons were smuggled into the ghetto by ghetto transport workers with the help of the Latvian Jewish ghetto police. Accompanied by Latvian SS guards, the transport workers came to the city with horse-drawn carts to collect food rations for the ghetto and also to bring food for the Jews living at their workplaces in the city. Dismantled rifles, machine guns, and ammunition were hidden in the crates and brought into the ghetto. Weapons, medicines, food, SS uniforms and insignia, and other essentials were procured and stored for use during the uprising.

Several elaborate bunkers were built, and a tunnel was started leading to a cemetery outside the ghetto. Although I did not know it, a bunker housing the weapons was located at 19 Vilanu Street under a shed in the backyard of the house next to our apartment. The entrance to the bunker was concealed in the wood-burning range in the kitchen. A second well-equipped bunker, concealed in an unoccupied dilapidated shack at the far edge of the ghetto, was prepared and stockpiled with food, medicines, and other essentials. The movement also established a clandestine firing range in a large cellar in the ghetto where men took instruction and practice in shooting.

Although the resistance movement had not been compromised, Bag and several other members were killed during the massacre of the Latvian Jewish ghetto police. The remaining members of the movement, under the leadership of Okun, decided to proceed with the preparations for armed resistance. Without the supportive presence and assistance of our own police, the whole operation, particularly the smuggling of weapons into the ghetto, became more hazardous. Nonetheless, the stockpiling of weapons and supplies continued, and dismantled guns, ammunition, and other items kept flowing into the ghetto.

After the incident on the highway, the Gestapo was alerted and tried to guard against an armed uprising in the ghetto. They had murdered the Latvian Jewish police to prevent a possible revolt in the Little Ghetto and replaced our slain policemen with German Jews who the Gestapo believed were more reliable, less likely to attempt a desperate rebellion. Many families of the German Jews were still alive, and those Jews had not witnessed the callous murders committed by the nazis during the evacuation of the Large Ghetto. Furthermore, in Riga the German Jews were much more isolated; they did not speak Latvian, and they had no knowledge of or contacts with the local community.

Roschmann set out to extract information from his recent captive, Israelowitz, who must have broken under torture. The resistance movement had been organized in small cells, and the members did not know the identity of most other participants. Although Israelowitz evidently did not know everything, he knew enough to start unraveling the entire scheme. In March 1943 the Gestapo brought Israelowitz into the ghetto, where he pointed out the location of a bunker containing supplies. It is thought that during their searches the nazis came across a list of members of the movement. Apparently operating from this list, the Gestapo arrested many persons during the next few months, always searching them out by name. In June 1943 they discovered the weapons bunker and arrested Okun, who lived in the apartment next to the bunker. In the car on his way to prison, Okun attacked Roschmann with a razor but only wounded him in the face.

The German Jewish replacement police were under the command of Friedrich Frankenberg and Rudolf Haar. Haar, a member of the German Jewish ghetto police, had once saved Commandant Krause's life. Krause had gotten into an argument with a Latvian SS guard, and the latter pointed his rifle at him. Haar, a former boxer, stepped in and tore the rifle from the guard. In appreciation, Krause promoted Haar to senior officer of the German Jewish ghetto police.

The Latvian Jews considered both Frankenberg and Haar henchmen of the nazis and did not trust them. Our suspicions were soon borne out. After the ghetto commandant had arrested one Botwinik, a locksmith who was a member of the resistance group, Frankenberg went to secure the arrested man's apartment. There he came upon a friend of Botwinik's, Eliaschewitz, who was trying to dispose of some incriminating evidence. Frankenberg arrested him and turned him over to the SS, who later executed him. The Latvian Jews believed Haar was also implicated, and we blamed both him and Frankenberg for denouncing Eliaschewitz. Haar steadfastly protested his innocence. A year later Haar was sent to the concentration camp Kaiserwald, where German criminal inmates drowned him in the latrine. Frankenberg was killed by Jewish fellow inmates in Buchenwald.

As a result of the weapons affair, several hundred people were killed. By November 1943 the Little Ghetto was disbanded, and the remaining inmates were sent to Kaiserwald, a concentration camp recently built on the outskirts of Riga. I was no longer living in the Little Ghetto. I had succeeded in finding a good work assignment where we were housed away from the ghetto.

WORK

In the Little Ghetto, which had been established as a working camp, we saw work as our ticket to survival. Conventional wisdom suggested that the nazis would not kill workers who were performing tasks important to Germany and contributing to the war effort. We were very much mistaken. The civilian Reichskommissar Ostland Hinrich Lohse did indeed object to killing Jews who were working in local war-related industries, but he was informed by his superiors at the Ministry of the Occupied Territories in Berlin that the needs of the war effort must not be considered in planning the fate of the Jews.[40] Although we were aware that the killings took place without regard to our work assignments, we still hoped some workers would escape death. It was incredible that the nazis might place less importance on the outcome of the war than on the extermination of the Jews. That, however, was exactly the case.

Each work unit generally had a Jewish foreman called Kollonen Führer (column leader) or Oberjude (chief or head Jew), who interacted with the German supervisors and in many cases (particularly for the more desirable assignments) selected the people working for him in the unit. The number of workers required on a job fluctuated, and the column leader was sometimes able to take on additional workers. Friendships and connections were important in securing better assignments. When the number of workers needed was reduced, some of us were dropped from that unit.

The workers in each unit were counted upon leaving and again upon reentering the ghetto, and the foreman was responsible for a correct count. Although our employers supposedly paid for our labor, we never saw any compensation. I repeatedly tried to find more desirable assignments. During my two years in the Little Ghetto I worked in a number of different places, sometimes for just a short time. My granduncle Artur Keilman, who after the loss of my father tried to be especially supportive, helped me secure several of the better assignments.

During the early months in the Little Ghetto I worked for Quartieramt, the Wehrmacht quartermaster, at the time one of the larger employers of Jews. We arranged and fixed up the quarters for army units and did janitorial and maintenance work. Occasionally, I worked directly for Wehrmacht units. I seldom stayed at one place longer than a few weeks, at most a month. Frequently, the units moved away from Riga. At other times the number of Jewish workers was reduced, and I was no longer needed. Sometimes, when I was able to find a better place to work, I left. After arranging with the leader of the new work unit, I would join his column and try to avoid being noticed by the group leader of the previous assignment.

Our German employers had no role in the administration of Jewish affairs. For them, the Jews were just a convenient and competent workforce. The German supervisors in charge of the Jewish workers, both from the Wehrmacht and occasionally even the SS, did establish limited personal relations with their Jewish employees, and some did try to protect those Jews from the selections, deportations, and killings occurring in the ghetto. Some used their positions to enrich themselves by extorting valuables from the Jews in return for promises of protection or preferential assignments. Corruption was rampant in nazi Germany, and we considered such demands a fact of life. The common German army slang referred to stealing as "organizing," and many officers and enlisted personnel of the SS and the Wehrmacht were constantly looking for opportunities for personal gain. As a rule, we much preferred corrupt officials to fanatic nazi ideologues—one could at least deal with the former. Even then, the critical question was whether the German could and would deliver on his part of the bargain. Such dealings with employers were common in Riga, both before and during the existence of the Large and Little Ghettos, although not in the concentration camps. In the camps our resources had dwindled, and our ability to access hidden valuables was curtailed. Furthermore, we were at the mercy of the SS, subject to the unlimited power and arbitrary whims of the camp commander and his henchmen. Even a hint of having something of value would trigger a violent expropriation attempt. Having nothing to negotiate with, our interactions with the overseers of the work assignments became entirely impersonal.

In midsummer 1942, shortly after the murder of Herr Kron, my granduncle Keilman helped me get a desirable assignment at the Riga Dairy, a work unit called Milch Fabrik (milk factory). The dairy, located just a few blocks from the ghetto, was a milk-product processing and distribution center for the output from provincial dairies. It had been nationalized by the Soviets when they occupied the country in July 1940. It was now run as a Latvian-owned enterprise and had no connection with the German military or civilian authorities.

Our column leader was David Berman. Berman had been in the dairy business prior to the war and used his connections to organize this work commando. The Ghetto Labor Office allocated Jewish workers. During the initial period of the Little Ghetto, a prospective employer could request Jewish workers by name, claiming they were familiar with the work and were therefore needed on the assignment. By negotiating with a friendly employer we were able to obtain a desirable work assignment.

The work detail at the Riga Dairy consisted of about thirty people. All of us worked side by side with the non-Jewish local civilian workers, most of whom were longtime employees at the dairy. Like them, we worked regular eight-hour days plus a half-day on Saturdays. I got along well with my coworkers.

My initial assignment was in the cottage cheese department. I was the only male working with about five Latvian women. The department received large cases of fat-free cottage cheese from out-of-town dairies and distributed it to various retail outlets. I was responsible for stacking the incoming cases of cottage cheese and later taking them out onto the loading dock and helping to load them on the deliverymen's horse-drawn wagons. The work was not too strenuous, and there were lulls during the day when I had some free time. The cottage cheese was not always fresh, but some cases were quite tasty. I ate as much as I wanted, but I never took any back to the ghetto.

My responsibilities included moving the empty cases to a shed in a storage area away from our department. I was sometimes assisted by a young Latvian coworker, Mirdza. She was a friendly, easygoing young woman about twenty years old. I liked her, and I liked to believe she also liked me. I would take a horse and wagon, and she would help me load on the empties and drive them to the storage area. I had fantasies about sleeping with Mirdza and entertained the hope that she would offer to hide me—a wild dream of sex and survival. Mirdza would, as it were, hide me in her bed. There was a complication—she shared her apartment with another of our coworkers who had a decidedly cool attitude toward me. I did not think Mirdza's roommate would agree to any such arrangement, and I never broached the idea.

I befriended several of the milkmen-salesmen. One of them was able to get fresh bread from a bakery, and he would occasionally sell me a loaf. I learned that the route of another deliveryman with whom I had established a friendly relationship included the Terminka Prison, where I believed my mother was being held. I asked him if he could make inquiries regarding her whereabouts. Several weeks later he reported that he had been told she had indeed been there until the night of January 15, 1942. He did not say what had happened to her, but in the context of the times it was not necessary. The implication was clear. It was now autumn 1942, more than a year since she had been detained. I was unsure what credence to attach to his information; it just confirmed my fears that my mother was dead.

Several months later I was transferred to the butter and cheese department. It was a better place to work because butter and cheese were more desirable products than cottage cheese. I worked with Berman, and we became good friends. In addition to Berman and myself, the workforce included several civilian workers: one young man and four women. I did much of the heavy lifting, although butter and cheese came in smaller boxes, which I could easily handle myself.

I especially liked one of the local civilian employees. Maria, an ethnic Russian in her mid-twenties, had worked in the department for some time. She was outspoken, strongly anti-German, and sympathetic to the plight of the Jews. She was interested to hear about our situation and deplored the anti-Semitic policies of the nazis and their Latvian sympathizers.

While working at the dairy we were able to move freely throughout the large plant. There was no surveillance, and except for being escorted to and from the ghetto, we could even leave the dairy at will. On one occasion I helped a young Latvian coworker collect her allotment of firewood and take it to her apartment. We borrowed a horse and wagon from the dairy, picked up the firewood at the distribution center, and took it to her place at the other end of the city. I went without the Jewish star. I was taking a foolhardy chance. It was an act of defiance; I did not consider the possible consequences. I just cherished a momentary sense of freedom, however fleeting.

After only seven months, in early 1943, our work unit at the dairy was discontinued. I was disappointed; it had been a very good assignment.

On my next work assignment I joined a small group working in a warehouse run by the German nazi party (NSDAP). The warehouse was a distribution center for sending gifts and special favors like liquor, cigars, cigarettes, chocolate, and other luxury items to the front line troops. We received and unloaded supplies, kept the warehouse in order, and packed crates. The warehouse was run by Herr Hauck, a Baltic German who diverted goods to his own use. The work commando consisted of about fifteen Jews, among them Joseph Bahn and Abram Lazar, men in their sixties who had used their connections and valuables to obtain this desirable assignment. Bahn and Lazar did the lighter work: unpacking, shelving the items. The younger men, myself included, did the heavier work: packing and lifting the crates and loading the trucks that came to pick up the gifts. It was a comfortable job. The work was not strenuous; we had a minimum of supervision and considerable freedom of movement.

One of the young women in the detail was a former classmate. Several times a week she cleaned our boss's apartment in the city, and I sometimes found a pretext to visit her there. A few times I was able to catch BBC broadcasts from London on the boss's radio, something strictly forbidden by the German authorities. Like the work at the dairy, this assignment was too good to last. In summer of 1943, after just five months, I again had to look for other work. It was safer to look for work myself than to depend on assignments from the Labor Office, which could result in very hard work under horrendous circumstances.

On some assignments the Jewish workers were kept overnight. This was a convenience to the employer and also benefited the workers, as it eliminated the daily round-trip from the ghetto to work and back. Staying overnight in town offered a more tranquil existence. The nightly ordeal of entering the Little Ghetto was risky at best. There was always a potential danger of being frisked for food or other forbidden items. The term used for living away from the ghetto near work was *Kasernierung* (being housed in barracks). Although being away from the ghetto was desirable, not all such arrangements were beneficent. Some were in killing camps, with backbreaking labor, starvation rations, and inhumane living conditions. Such was the case with work assignments to peat bogs, from which few returned. The critical advantage of staying away from the ghetto became evident during the nights of the *Aktion* when the Large Ghetto was liquidated. Later, when more and more people from both the Little and the Reichsjuden Ghettos were being sent to Kaiserwald, it became clear that the ghetto would soon be closed. I tried to find assignments with local living arrangements in the city to avoid being shipped to Kaiserwald.

With the help of friends I was fortunate soon to find work at HKP (Heereskraftfahrpark), an army motor pool and maintenance facility. I had previously worked there for a short time and knew the Jewish foreman of the unit. This work unit had started even before the destruction of the Large Ghetto, and its Jewish foreman had established good relations with the German major in charge of the HKP. A small group of the Jewish workers lived in the central facility starting in early autumn of 1941, whereas others were trucked daily back and forth to the ghetto.

The Jewish workers were under the control of Obergefreiter (private first class) Walter Eggers of Hamburg. Eggers used his position to take bribes from wealthy people who were willing to pay handsomely for the privilege of living at the facility, and he was able to amass a considerable fortune. A few wealthy Jews managed to work there, as did a number of skilled artisans. The *Kasernierung* at HKP helped several families survive the big *Aktion* during the liquidation of the Large Ghetto. Among them were two girls I knew from school and their families.

During summer of 1943, when I started to work at HKP, I was still living in the Little Ghetto. Although I was not a mechanic I was assigned to the truck repair department, where I performed maintenance and other manual tasks. Our work was not hard, and the general atmosphere was relaxed. The SS and Gestapo leadership from the ghetto, and later from the concentration camp Kaiserwald, heard rumors about the good life at HKP and showed increasing interest in the work unit. Even though our German supervisors occasionally tried to intervene and shield us, raids and searches took place, and several Jews were arrested.

A few months later, in early fall of 1943, the liquidation of the Little Ghetto appeared imminent. A *Kasernierung* was arranged for us in a large two-story garage on Wasserstrasse (Water Street) in Pardaugava, the Riga suburb across the River Daugava. The upper floor of the garage was converted to a barracks-like facility with separate dormitories and washrooms for men and women. The men's dormitory housed about 200 people, but the women's section was much smaller. We were taken by truck to work each day at the main facility. We slept in three-story bunks with straw mattresses. I occupied an uppermost bunk at one end of the dormitory. Nine of us shared this corner, which had a separate entry. Even though our bunks abutted those of the large dormitory, we had a little more privacy than was available in the main section.

At HKP I again met up with my friend Mulya Atlas, who took the bunk below me. A father and son Levine also stayed in this area. The son, Alexander (Lexi), was the same age as I. He had a girlfriend, Lily Kreutzer, a stunningly beautiful girl who spent weekends with him in our corner. We were a congenial and friendly group. Sometimes we had small celebrations and drank vodka, which was readily available. I recall one time I drank too much and retired to my bunk. I kept complaining that the bunk was swaying, which amused my comrades no end. Lily and I became good friends, but I did not try to compete for her affections.

Hiding Our Wealth – A Resource in the Struggle for Survival

It was common practice among Jews to bury or otherwise hide their valuables—gold, precious jewelry, or foreign currency—to avoid confiscation and loss and to have it available in case it was needed to ensure survival. Some entrusted their property to gentile friends or acquaintances for safekeeping. Unfortunately, these friends often proved unreliable. People sometimes denounced their friends to the authorities to keep the property for themselves. Under the circumstances, burying valuables seemed safer, particularly for gold coins and items of jewelry that could be easily hidden. Finding a site that would remain undisturbed and permit easy retrieval was problematic. After we were locked into the ghetto, people buried their treasure right inside the ghetto. Following the liquidation of the Large Ghetto, many people—Germans, Latvians, and Jews from the Little Ghetto—combed the now vacant ghetto area for hidden hoards. Many valuables were unearthed there, and sporadic discoveries will no doubt continue to be made for years to come.

Just before moving to the ghetto, my father had hidden a suitcase with clothing in the attic of a small cottage on a parcel of land we owned in Sarkandaugava, a poor industrial area not far from our factory. My father had sewn some of my mother's diamonds in a piece of clothing. I had met the man living there but did not know him well and was not sure I could trust him. Unless he had searched the suitcase, he probably did not know about the diamonds. Still, like many others, he may have wanted to keep our possessions and could have denounced me to the Gestapo. I did not want to risk it, and while in the Little Ghetto I made no effort to retrieve the hidden diamonds.

My father also told me he had buried some gold coins and foreign banknotes in a glass jar near the villa in Jurmala we had rented in the summer of 1939. He described the hiding place, outside the villa near its foundation, in detail. For most of the year the villa was uninhabited, making it relatively easy to retrieve the hoard. When I was in the Little Ghetto I decided to do so but could not arrange a trip to Jurmala. My cousin Mako, however, worked at the Feldkommandatur (Army Field Command) and was able to find someone willing to take him there. Mako agreed to try to get the valuables with the understanding that we would share in the proceeds. For a while I heard nothing from him. Then he told me he had not been able to arrange the trip. Next he reported that he had gone there but had not found anything. When I persisted, he changed his story: he had found only some worthless, small-denomination foreign banknotes, which he returned to me. I was convinced that he had also found the gold coins but that he kept them. I never expected that he would steal from me, and I complained to my uncle Keilman, but to no avail. Paul Dawidson, who knew our cousin Mako was not a truthful or trustworthy person, commiserated with me.

POSSIBILITIES OF ESCAPE AND SUPPORT BY THE LATVIAN COMMUNITY

The tide of war had turned decisively in January 1943 with the disastrous defeat the Red Army inflicted on the Germans at Stalingrad. From that point on there was little doubt about the eventual outcome of the war. The question shifted from *if* the Germans would be defeated to *when*. By late winter and spring of 1944 their defeat was a foregone conclusion, and even the Germans seemed to know it. We listened gleefully to stories told by friends who worked near the railroad, stories of trains returning from the front loaded with casualties—people with missing arms, legs, and heads. The certainty of Germany's defeat buoyed my morale greatly, but it was not clear whether I would survive to see it.

At HKP our living conditions were relatively bearable, and we could still supplement our meager rations. There were recurrent searches and arrests, and those kept us off balance and made the atmosphere tense. The threat of being taken to Kaiserwald grew ever more serious and weighed heavily on our minds. The starvation and brutal conditions at the camp were common knowledge, and we knew that sooner or later we would end up there. As the end of our stay at Wasserstrasse approached, several persons managed to escape. For every escapee, hostages were taken and sent to Kaiserwald. Still, some managed to slip away undetected and were not missed.

I heard rumors about a Latvian who was prepared to give shelter to a number of Jews, but I was not able to obtain his address. At the time I was convinced that the escapees paid handsomely for being sheltered. Surrounded by corruption, it was inconceivable to me that anyone would offer to save Jews without a payment or bribe. Not having any valuables I did not pursue the matter. As it turned out, I was wrong. After the war I learned that the rescuer, Janis Lipke, did not turn away any Jew who appeared at his door or demand any payment or compensation for his help. Lipke with his wife, Johanna, and two helpers saved as many as sixty people. Several of my coworkers, including Lexi and Lily, were among them. Lipke has been honored by Yad Vashem as a Righteous Gentile (a gentile who helped save Jews during the Holocaust).

Although I had never discussed it with my father, thoughts of escape, resistance, and going into hiding were frequently on my mind. Escaping from the Little Ghetto was simple; the difficulty lay in finding a place to hide. Although an Allied victory seemed assured, liberation might be months off. To have any hope for success, I was going to need a safe place and a reliable support system.

I believe Paulina Streipa could have been of help to me during the nazi occupation. She was a knowledgeable person, and I think she had connections in Latvian society. Her son-in-law was a lawyer. Paulina did seek me out hoping to find out what had happened to Eduard, but she did not offer any help. I did not like or trust her and did not ask her for anything.

Our former cook Anna might have helped, but I did not think she had the wherewithal to do so. She left our employment during the Russian occupation in 1940 and moved into a one-room basement apartment, which she shared with her elderly aunt. I never heard from her during the more than three years of nazi occupation in which I remained in Riga, and I did not try to contact her. Anna's apartment was tiny; there was not enough room for creating a safe hideout. Unlike Paulina Streipa, who knew how to find me, I considered Anna too unsophisticated to get in touch with me, let alone manage such an undertaking. Not expecting more from Anna, I was not disappointed by her failure to help me.

To my knowledge, none of the people from our factory tried to contact my father, and nobody reached out to me. I had only a nodding acquaintance with some of the supervisors and workers. I had no Latvian friends, let alone anyone I could trust. After the war, Leo was incredulous to hear that none of his close Latvian friends had made an effort on behalf of our family or come forward with an offer to help. He named Ludolfs Liberts, the painter, and Janis Jaunsudrabiņš, the writer, as well as several others. Each time I had to tell him "no, he did not contact us." Leo could not accept that his longtime Latvian friends were anti-Semites. I, however, had no such trouble. Our disagreement over the actions and behavior of the

Latvians during the German occupation was the one serious issue Leo and I were never able to resolve.

My Jewish friends who had escaped to the Soviet Union also perceived the Latvians very differently. In the Soviet Union they were thrown together with Latvian refugees. Latvian Jews served in a Latvian division in the Red Army. Together with Latvian gentiles they had fought against the nazis and developed a sense of camaraderie. My friends never witnessed the gratuitous barbarism perpetrated by Latvians. They blame only Latvian fascists for the atrocities. To us, survivors from the ghettos and camps, this seems incomprehensible.

In other European nations—the Netherlands, Czechoslovakia, and, most notably, Denmark and Bulgaria—there were people who tried to save Jews. In Latvia, however, the number of Righteous Gentiles was painfully small. Fear of the Germans was certainly a contributing factor. Several Latvians who were hiding Jews were denounced to the Gestapo by their neighbors. The captured Jews as well as the would-be rescuers were summarily shot. Another significant element was the social and cultural distance between the two communities. Not speaking the same language, not having a bond of common interests or a sense of shared destiny reduced the interaction between Latvians and Jews and limited the number of close relationships that could have led to attempts of support and rescue. With the notable exception of the Janis and Johanna Lipkes, no more than a handful of people risked their lives to help their Jewish neighbors and friends.

The history of Latvia, long years of serfdom and a succession of foreign rulers—Germans, Swedes, Poles, and Russians—may have conditioned Latvians to obey the rules and commands imposed on them by their current masters. Independent Latvia was created after World War I with the support of the Western Allies as a buffer against communism. As the West's (notably Britain's) ability to guarantee Latvia's independence diminished, the Baltic republics increasingly found themselves at the mercy of their two large neighbors, Germany and Russia. The Latvians (as well as citizens of the other Baltic countries) were unwilling to make common cause with their neighbors or their own minorities. The Latvians made no realistic attempt to fight or to control their own destiny or to help their Jewish compatriots escape from theirs. As Anatol Lieven observed about Lithuania, but equally applicable to the situation in Latvia:

> With two peoples, living in the same land but obeying the dictates of
> opposed national priorities, ignorant of each other's culture, indifferent
> to each other's interests, and in an atmosphere in which anti-semitism
> was fed by Nazi propaganda as well as by indigenous prejudice, the stage
> was set for catastrophe.[41]

I still vividly recall the words spoken to me by an elderly Latvian woman. She saw me, a total stranger, in the city a few days after the destruction of the Large Ghetto and said, "Soon they are going to kill you all." She was just stating a fact. She was only a bystander, and there was nothing she could or would try to do about it. I was taken aback by the bluntness of her words. I had not yet accepted that the so-called resettlement had been a killing, that the majority of my fellow Jews in the Large Ghetto had been murdered. I did not expect an offer of help from a stranger, but I would have welcomed an expression of empathy, of her loathing of the callous killings. Her remarks confirmed my perception that I could expect no help from the Latvian population.

A memoir by the Latvian American writer Agate Nesaule, *A Woman in Amber,* casts some light on the attitude of Latvians toward the Holocaust. In 1944, to escape the advancing Red Army, Nesaule's family, together with many other Latvians, chose to leave with the retreating Wehrmacht. Nesaule tells of an incident in Germany just after the war, where her mother pushed her two young daughters to the head of a group of German and refugee women and children. The mother thought they all were about to be shot by the Russian soldiers and tried to save her daughters the agony of seeing the others killed while waiting for their turn. Nesaule never forgave her mother for what she interpreted as trying to get her killed. To me, however, the mother's fears give a clue to her thinking. Like most Latvians, killers and passive bystanders alike, she knew of and understood the heinous crimes perpetrated by her countrymen immediately upon the German occupation in summer of 1941. Latvians had systematically murdered Jewish men, women, and children. Nesaule's mother was convinced that the same fate would now befall her and her children. She could not even conceive that the Soviets would treat them any differently.[42]

As it turned out, unlike the situation in Germany proper, the Red Army treated the Baltics as liberated territories and handled the civilian population there with relative constraint. Still, however disingenuous it may be, the Latvians are fond of portraying themselves as the innocent victims of Russian aggression.

I thought of joining the partisans. The nearest area of resistance was in the forests of Byelorussia, south and southeast of Dvinsk. Getting there presented insurmountable difficulties. In fact, the weapons affair in the Little Ghetto had started with an abortive attempt by some Jews to join the partisans. Sweden, just 100 kilometers across the Baltic Sea, was another beacon of hope that proved just a mirage. One episode showed how impossible it was to reach that safe haven from Latvia. At a workplace in Riga, some Jews from the ghetto, including attorney Jewelson, came to know a Luftwaffe lieutenant. He seemed helpful and supportive, gained their confidence, and offered to arrange for their departure to Sweden. It turned out that they had fallen prey to a Gestapo provocation. Having paid for the trip with gold and jewels, they boarded the ship where they were greeted by Ghetto Commander Krause. They all were subsequently killed.[43]

Although we did not know that in June 1943 Himmler had ordered the liquidation of all ghettos, we were aware of a mounting insistence by the SS to move all Jews into concentration camps.[44] The construction of KZ Kaiserwald (KZ is the German abbreviation for concentration camp) in Mežaparks had begun in early 1943. Ironically, this was the suburb where our family had lived just prior to the German occupation. (Kaiserwald is the German name for that suburb.) By July of that year, the first groups of people from our ghetto were being shipped there. The SS administration of Kaiserwald took over management of the affairs of all Jews in the Riga area, including the ghetto and the various *Kasernierungen.* We knew about Kaiserwald and the terrible conditions prevailing there. It also became clear that the days of the Little Ghetto were numbered.

The Riga ghettos, both the Reichsjuden Ghetto and the Little Ghetto, were finally emptied in November 1943 in an *Aktion* reminiscent of the liquidation of the Large Ghetto two years earlier. A selection took place, and the remaining elderly and children, mostly from the Reichsjuden Ghetto, were grabbed for deportation. Many of the children taken were alone because their parents were away at work. The SS flushed them from their ghetto hiding places, drove them out onto the street, and threw them into waiting trucks. Among the children were some who had survived the earlier liquidation of the Large Ghetto. The children and elderly were locked into freight cars and shipped off to be killed at Auschwitz.[45]

I worked at HKP for about a year. Living in the barracks on Wasserstrasse, I managed to evade the final liquidation of the Little Ghetto and to postpone being shipped to Kaiserwald until early August 1944. The Red Army advanced westward slowly but steadily, and the front was at last approaching Riga. As part of the retreat and evacuation planned by the Germans, the work detail at HKP was eliminated, and Wasserstrasse was closed. Crammed onto trucks, the Jewish workers were taken to Kaiserwald.

18
KZ Kaiserwald

After a short truck ride through Riga we arrived at Kaiserwald, the feared camp I had tried so long to avoid. We were met by SS men who ordered us off the truck shouting *"schneller, schneller"* (faster, faster). Pushed and prodded with sticks and truncheons by German and Polish inmates, we were driven into and out of showers so quickly we barely had a chance to get wet. Striped prisoners' pajamas were thrust at us. We always had to move on the run—to and from the showers, to and from roll call, to and from the barracks, and so on—constantly dodging jabs and indiscriminate blows while the guards and *Kapos* (in concentration camp argot a privileged inmate or trustee, usually a gentile, used to control other inmates) screamed *"schneller, schneller!"*

In the concentration camps, as part of the systematic degradation we also lost our names—in Kaiserwald I became prisoner No. 10021. Our numbers were imprinted on small rectangles of white cloth on the left breast next to an identifying triangle. Jews had a yellow triangle, criminals green, and political prisoners red. To complicate chances for escape, diagonal white crosses were painted on the fronts and backs of our jackets. Stripes adorned the sides of our pants. We were issued round visor-less caps, which we had to doff smartly to salute any SS who passed.

Concentration camp Kaiserwald was a complex of a number of barracks organized into three separate sections. The first, at the main gate, was the administrative section, which housed the SS staff and the guards. The guards generally were non-German SS troops—Latvian, Ukrainian, or Lithuanian. We had little contact with the guards except when they accompanied inmates on outside work details. Behind the administrative building were the women's and men's sections, separated by double rows of barbed wire fence. Construction of the camp had started in early 1943, using inmates from other camps. Five hundred gentile prisoners had been imported from concentration camp Sachsenhausen for this purpose. They worked and lived under terrible conditions. When Jews from the Riga ghettos started to arrive in late summer of 1943, only 60 percent of the original inmates were still alive.[46]

Kaiserwald was under the command of Obersturmbannführer (colonel) Albert Sauer, previously a construction entrepreneur from Berlin. He had a staff of German SS but relied heavily on German political and criminal inmates for the internal administration of the camp. We already knew many of the German SS from the ghetto and other camps, where they had earned a well-deserved reputation as murderers. The German SS were very visible in the camp. They verified the results of the head count during roll calls and often strolled through the camp looking for an opportunity to amuse themselves by making trouble. Heading the hierarchy of inmates was the Lagerältester (head or senior of the camp), usually a German criminal or political prisoner. The Germans, both men and women, constituted an aristocracy among camp inmates. Many of the men were career criminals (*Berufs Verbrecher*), and most of the women were convicted prostitutes. These women, placed in charge of the women's camp, continued to ply their trade, drawing their clientele from among the SS and the German inmates. Ranking below the Germans were the Polish and Ukrainian inmates. At the bottom of the pecking order, receiving all of the abuse and beatings but very little food, were the Jews.

My recollections of Kaiserwald are not as clear as those from the ghetto. I stayed in Kaiserwald about six weeks, but the immutable routine of the camp made all days seem alike. The daily routine started with wake-up shouts at 4 A.M. and roll call at 5 A.M. I remember mostly the interminable roll calls, the cramped barracks, and the narrow bunks that made sleeping a nightmare. The roll calls, mornings and evenings, involved repeated counting of inmates and were intentionally arranged to cause maximum harassment and discomfort. While standing at attention for hours we were counted, recounted, and counted again. If the counts did not agree (and frequently they did not), we were counted over and over, all the time required to stand at attention. There were repeated commands of "caps off" and "caps on." If these moves were not executed smartly to the liking of the SS, we were punished by being required to squat and remain in that painful position for an extended period. Everything was intended to make our existence as unendurable as possible.

The nazis deliberately encouraged brutality, rewarding the most vicious among the criminal inmates with promotion to *Kapo* and other camp perks. It would be hard to conceive of a more sadistically cruel assortment of misfits. One of the most notorious offenders was Xavier Apel from Berlin, known to us as Mister X, who was serving a life sentence for double murder. Max Kaufman describes Apel's routine in the camp:

He was a slender, handsome man, and everyone in the camp trembled in his presence. Whenever he joined an outside work detail as its leader, he would regularly return to camp with many dead or half-dead inmates. This elegant criminal had uncounted murders on his conscience. As a consequence he met a bad end. He was murdered by the inmates shortly before the liberation in Stutthof. After the evacuation from Riga, he had been working there [in Stutthof] in the Labor Office.[47]

Jews who exhibited brutal or even sadistic streaks were sometimes promoted to Block Ältester (block or barracks supervisor or leader). An atmosphere of casual violence and cruelty—incessantly fostered by the SS—corrupted everyone in the camp system, perpetrators and victims alike. Preoccupied with our own survival, we were oblivious to the pain of our fellow sufferers. There was no empathy for others who got into difficulties. I felt nothing; I was not affected. I just stepped aside and hoped I would not get into similar trouble. In fact, any display of human consideration or attempt to help one's fellows would trigger an immediate assault by the SS.

One group of Jews who reached prominent status in my barracks was a gang of young men from Poland, originally from the Jewish underworld of Lodz. This Mafia-like clique had been in ghettos and camps since the German invasion of Poland in 1939. It was rumored that the leaders of the Lodz Ghetto had marked these men for resettlement as a way of ridding themselves of the local criminal element. Their leader was a certain Ignatz who did not so much talk as scream curses in Polish-accented Yiddish. He often beat his fellow prisoners with a vehemence that made him indistinguishable from the Polish *Kapos*.

We lived in large dormitory barracks, about 300 inmates in each, where we were constantly under the baleful eyes of a *Kapo*. Violence and brutality were the norm. We were beaten when scrambling to get out through the narrow doorway of the barracks in the morning and again when crowding back in at night. We slept three abreast in three-tiered bunks, squeezed together on one narrow pallet with its small straw mattress, usually two facing one way and the third the other. I have a recollection of always having somebody's smelly feet in my face. Our boots served as pillows—not for comfort but to keep them from being stolen off our feet while we slept. Socks were unavailable; mine had long since disintegrated. I had mended them repeatedly until there was not enough sock left to darn. My friend Mulya Atlas had taught me how to wrap foot wraps instead; these were large rectangular cotton cloths, wound around our feet and worn inside the boots. They were used by the Soviet soldiers. It was rather efficient footwear, readily washed and, if carefully wrapped, comfortable and suitable for keeping one's feet well cared for.

My most valued and indispensable possessions were a canteen and spoon. Without them there would have been no way to collect the daily ration of soup. The so-called soup was a lukewarm opaque liquid with an occasional floating potato or piece of cabbage. The rations for the Jewish prisoners were much more minimal than those for the German and other gentile inmates. They were deliberately set at starvation level. We got about a half pound of bread daily (one third or one quarter of a loaf), with a pat of oleomargarine or marmalade. The diet soon caused our legs to swell, particularly around the ankles. Every day I anxiously examined my feet and legs for this feared sign of malnutrition. Under the circumstances, an extra portion of soup was a gift from heaven. We devised all kinds of stratagems to get one, such as running errands for the *Kapo* or carrying the soup kettles from the kitchen to the barracks.

A particularly odious scourge of the camps was the ever-present lice. I had not had lice in the ghetto or at HKP, but I was infested as soon as I came to Kaiserwald. I tried in vain to keep clean, but the facilities for personal hygiene were utterly inadequate. My feeble attempts to control the lice were a losing battle. Whenever malnutrition was complemented by an inability to keep clean, lice seemed to materialize as if by spontaneous generation. Close physical contact with other inmates in the congested quarters of our barracks made it impossible to avoid being inundated by lice. The Germans did not have DDT, and the occasional superficial showers and steam sanitizing of our clothes did nothing to control the infestation. Even after liberation, when all my camp clothing had been burned, it took repeated washing and scrubbing before I rid myself of the last traces of these vermin.

While at Kaiserwald I worked in several different places, although I do not recall many details. Several times I unloaded ships in the port of Riga. In the holds we sometimes found food and were occasionally out of the immediate view of the *Kapos.*

As the Red Army advanced toward Riga from the east, the nazis sought to destroy evidence of the atrocities they had committed three years earlier. Jewish inmates were sent to work for SS Stützpunkt (support center), an outfit assigned to dig up the dead, search them for hidden valuables like gold or jewelry, and burn the corpses. Selection to Stützpunkt was a death sentence. After working in chains for a couple of weeks, the workers were killed. No one returned or escaped from this assignment. My friend from HKP, Leo Neuburger, was selected to the Stützpunkt commando immediately upon arrival in Kaiserwald. I can still see him being hauled into a covered truck with his leg dangling over the tailgate. Neuburger was a shrewd man in his mid-forties who had managed to stay alive through many difficult situations. Seeing him being dragged to his death was shocking; even a man as canny as Neuburger had no chance of surviving. I suspect Neuburger may have been denounced to the SS by someone who had dealt with him and now found it expedient to be rid of him. Dealings with the Germans were always risky and could backfire disastrously.

The first evacuation of inmates from Kaiserwald to Germany occurred on August 6, 1944, just prior to my arrival at the camp. The second and final evacuation of the camp started late on Yom Kippur eve, September 26, 1944, just as the Red Army was closing in on Riga. We were taken by truck to the port and were kept standing dockside, awaiting orders to move onto the ship. We knew we were going to Germany but not to which port. Embarkation in the export port of Riga was a scene of utter confusion that lasted well into dark; our ship did not leave port until late at night. While we were on the dock, few guards were in evidence. We were not standing in an orderly fashion but were milling around freely. As dusk started to descend I seriously contemplated escaping. The escape would have been easy; I could literally have just walked away. On the one hand, I knew the city intimately and was sure it would soon fall to the Soviets. On the other hand, soon might not be soon enough. It might easily take another month. With nobody I could rely on for support and no hiding place, I decided not to escape. Three weeks after our departure, on October 13, 1944, the Red Army recaptured Riga.

19
KZ Stutthof

We were locked in the cargo holds of the freighter for the duration of the voyage. With the hatches covered and no sanitary facilities available, the foul, stifling air in the holds grew ever more rank. There was no water in the holds, and we suffered miserably from thirst. At one point we were "given" water by having a high-pressure fire hose turned on us. I think it was potable water, but we could not collect enough to assuage our thirst. We did not know where we were headed or when we would arrive. We were concerned that the Germans would scuttle the ship. Our anxiety grew until the fourth day, when we arrived in the port of Danzig (present-day Gdansk in Poland). Here we were transferred to river barges, bulk carriers normally intended for carrying cement or coal. Again there was no water. After being towed about half a day, we arrived at our destination: the KZ Stutthof.

We were driven from the barges and herded into the camp and barracks under a hail of blows, accompanied by a steady refrain of shouts from the Polish inmates: "*Ale jusz, ale jeszcze*" (literally "now already, now again," meaning "move faster, faster"). There was a large Polish presence among the inmates and *Kapos,* and much of the shouting was in Polish. In Stutthof my identity changed. I ceased being prisoner 10021 and became prisoner No. 96211, but unlike at Auschwitz, in Stutthof our numbers were not tattooed on our arms.*

---

*I recently received information from the Stutthof Museum in Poland about my concentration camp record. Even though we were known by just our numbers, the nazis kept meticulous accounts of the prisoners. My record includes my birth date, mother's name, and dates of arrival and departure from the camp. The records from KZ Kaiserwald and the Riga ghettos have not been found. The SS must have destroyed them when they evacuated Riga.

Stutthof was a vast camp with a large number of barracks. Kaiserwald was dwarfed by comparison. The larger size also magnified the violence and brutality. The daily routine was similar to that of Kaiserwald, except here it was frequently punctuated by violent interruptions. Public hangings and occasional selections added a dimension of terror to the monotony. I recall being forced to witness the hanging of two prisoners. Their alleged infraction was announced over loudspeakers, but exactly what they were supposed to have done was not clear to me. I understood that the men were being executed on some trumped-up pretext and that I was about to witness yet another nazi obscenity. The gallows had been erected in the central square of the camp, called the parade grounds. All prisoners were marched there and kept at attention for a long time. Just before the execution the command "caps off" was issued.

Among its various facilities Stutthof had a gas chamber and a crematorium, although they were smaller than those in the extermination camps. The Stutthof gas chamber never achieved the killing capacity of Auschwitz. Nevertheless, death rates from malnutrition and disease, mostly typhoid fever and dysentery, were staggering.[48] The food was inadequate and terrible: a quarter of a loaf of bread, dark brown water—called coffee—in the morning, and watery soup with a piece of rotten potato or a floating leaf of cabbage at night. It was a starvation diet, deliberately planned to kill us from malnutrition and disease. Unlike in Riga, where we had been able to get some additional food to supplement our rations, in Stutthof we had no such opportunities. I first encountered the so-called Muselmänner (literally "Moslems"), the concentration camp term for completely emaciated persons, walking skeletons. I do not recall many details of my stay in the camp, but the gnawing hunger, endless roll calls, and ever-present fear and anxiety remain irrevocably etched in my mind.

Inmates were periodically subjected to selections where unfit individuals, mainly the elderly and those who looked sick, were "selected" for the crematorium or for transfer to Auschwitz. The selections were made by camp SS officers, either during routine roll calls or at roll calls held especially for that purpose. To minimize the chance of being singled out during the selections, we tried to be shaved and to look as fit as possible. Shaving was difficult. What razors we had were dull; it was more like scraping off our beards. The older men tried particularly hard to appear as young as possible. They also sought to be inconspicuous during roll call by standing in the back row, preferably behind some taller person. No matter how sick a person might be, he tried desperately to avoid being sent to the infirmary, which was periodically emptied and its inmates sent to the crematorium.

In Stutthof I did not work. We were kept standing in endless roll calls, two to three hours in the morning and again in the evening. Communal

MUZEUM

STUTTHOF

Sztutowo 1998.08.13

W SZTUTOWIE

82-110 Sztutowo
woj. Elbląskie
tel. 8353
fax 83 58
Oddział Muzeum Stutthof
81-703 Sopot
ul. Kościuszki 63
tel. 51-29-87

L.dz. 1425/155/98

Pan
Max MICHELSON
26 Ridgefield Dr
RRAMINGHAM, MASSACHUSETTS 01701

Państwowe Muzeum Stutthof w Sztutowie stwierdza, że w materiałach dokumentalnych tutejszego Archiwum są następujące dane o niżej wymienionym więźniu byłego obozu koncentracyjnego Stutthof:

MICHELSON Max ur. 2.10.1924r. w Rydze, i. matki Erna, dostarczony został do KL Stutthof w dniu 1.10.1944 przez Sipo Ryga. W obozie oznaczony numerem **96 221** jako więzień polityczny. Dnia 3.11.1944r. przeniesiony został do KL Buchenwald.

Innych danych o w/w Muzeum nie posiada.
PODSTAWA informacji: I-III-32 999 Karta personalna więźnia.
/ka/

DYREKTOR

mgr Janina Grabowska-Chałka

Information about my records in Stutthof.

punishment was freely and frequently administered. Whatever the transgression, we were all made to squat, a position that becomes very painful if maintained for any length of time.

After the morning roll call had finally ended, we were not permitted back into our barracks. Instead we milled around outside during the day. It was autumn, and the days were cold. We would try to warm ourselves by forming what we called a chimney. Standing huddled together against the side of the barracks best protected from the wind, we tried to gain some heat from one another. We would stand there for hours in a mindless vegetative state that was undoubtedly a symptom of malnutrition. The endless hours of numbing boredom dragged on, making each day seem interminable. I lost all sense of time. The days flowed indistinguishably one into another, and weeks passed imperceptibly. I was lucky: in early November I was sent by train, crammed in the inevitable boxcars, to Magdeburg in Germany. I had been in Stutthof for just five weeks, more than enough for a lifetime.

20

Polte-Werke—Magdeburg

We arrived in Magdeburg and were immediately installed in a small slave labor camp attached to a munitions factory—Polte-Werke. In our part of the camp 500 inmates, mostly from Riga, were housed in two barracks. The camp was under the jurisdiction of KZ Buchenwald and was administered by the SS. Our commandant was Hoffman, and his assistant was Schuller. Both of these Germans had been on the SS staff of the commandant of KZ Kaiserwald, where they had been notorious for killing and beating inmates. I received a Buchenwald number: 95985.* Unlike our stay at Stutthof, we now were working, but otherwise our situation was unchanged—we were still on a starvation diet. At Polte we worked twelve-hour shifts six days a week, alternating every other week between day and night shifts. The plant directly adjoined the camp, and from our barracks it was only a short march to the factory.

At the factory I was assigned to a vertical extrusion press drawing 5-inch-diameter artillery shell casings. The process started with a thick disc, first formed to a deep cup and then repeatedly extruded to make the shell casing. I was working on the final extrusion operation, drawing the shell from about a 1-foot length to the final 3-foot length. The die was not supposed to have any scratches because any marks would score the shell and make it a reject. To aid in the extrusion operation the shell was soaked in a tub of soapy lubricant. Placing the shell in the extrusion press required a rhythmic motion. I would take it from the lubricant bath and place it under the piston. The machine operated at a continuous pace, and I had to work

---

*After the unification of Germany the records from KZ Buchenwald became public, and I was able to obtain a copy of my file. To my surprise I am listed as an automobile mechanic.

in step with the cycle of the press, always inserting the next piece before the piston descended. It was dangerous work. I had to be constantly alert and keep up with the movement of the piston. Inserting the shell sideways would cause the full force of the piston to hit the work broadside, damaging the machine and potentially injuring the operator.

I worked with a German master. Even after several months of being together during the twelve-hour shifts, we did not develop a personal relationship. He may not have been a bad person. Occasionally, if I did something wrong, he became irritated, but unlike some of the other masters, he never hit me. Beyond instructing me about my assignment, we never talked. In previous contacts with Germans, mostly civilians and Wehrmacht soldiers but even some SS men, they had frequently shown casual interest and asked questions about my situation in particular and about Jews in general. I found my master's attitude unusual and disturbing and resented being treated like a nonperson. For lunch I received the usual watery soup while he unwrapped his carefully packed sandwich and ate it without ever throwing me a crumb. He did not wear the party insignia and probably was not a nazi party member. But as far as I was concerned he was not human, just a nazi bastard.

Each of the two men's barracks housed members of one of the shifts. The leader of one of the barracks was Ignatz, originally from the Lodz ghetto. The professional skills Ignatz had acquired in the Lodz underworld before the war made him uniquely qualified to operate effectively in the corrupt camp environment. I had met him in Kaiserwald and quickly learned to give him as wide a berth as possible. At Magdeburg he surrounded himself with a gang of friends and cronies, many of whom were his long-time criminal associates. I was lucky to live in the other barracks with another leader whose name I do not remember.

Our Jewish camp leader was David Kagan, a former boxer who was also from Riga. We had met in the Little Ghetto and had worked together at the Riga Dairy. In his book Max Kaufman describes Kagan as a sadist who made our lives miserable. My recollections do not bear this out. Kagan used his hands freely and could occasionally be fairly brutal. He could be relied upon when it really mattered, however, to use his limited power to protect other Jews. In the United States after the war, some former Polte prisoners charged Kagan with maltreating his fellow inmates. He was accused of having beaten a prisoner caught stealing bread from his coworkers. Many of us, including myself, submitted affidavits on Kagan's behalf. The issue as I saw it was not simply whether he beat an inmate (I don't doubt that he did), but I felt a person who stole bread from his fellow inmates deserved to be beaten, and time has done nothing to change my mind. Bread was a matter of life and death, and stealing bread from a fellow prisoner was a capital offense.

Food had become an obsession, and to get it I was willing to take tremendous risks. In February I was caught stealing potato peels. There was a kitchen not far from the factory hall where I worked, and potato peels and other kitchen refuse were discarded outside. Several times I managed to slip undetected through the window of the adjacent men's room and scavenge potato peels and an occasional carrot. One time I was not so lucky: a camp guard noticed me outside. By the time he stormed into the room, I had reentered the bathroom and was sitting on the commode. I claimed somebody else had just jumped through the window and run away. I was hauled before Hoffman, our camp commandant, who beat me while I loudly and steadfastly maintained my innocence. They might have beaten me to death trying to make me confess, but if I did confess they would surely have killed me. Eventually, Kagan intervened. He managed to stop the beating by suggesting to Hoffman that apparently I really did not know who the culprit had been. I am convinced that Kagan saved my life.

After this episode I vowed that if I were lucky enough to return to a normal life, I would never again eat potato peels. Even though I try hard to comply with my vow, I have had some difficulty keeping it. Potatoes are a wonderful food; I love them and have them frequently. With baked potatoes in particular, even the skins are delicious. They are nothing like the rotten, discarded peels I had in mind when I resolved never to eat them again. When I occasionally do eat some of the skin, I feel guilty for not adhering to my vow.

Another incident involved my classmate from elementary school, Hank Bermanis, who worked as an electrician. To disrupt the operation of the ammunition factory, Hank sabotaged the freight elevator that served as the sole transportation link between the main and second floors of our factory building. He reversed the electrical connections so that when the elevator was next used, it drove into the stops and was severely damaged. Although we could not assess the overall effect of Hank's daring action, the smooth flow of material on the shop floor was noticeably delayed. To protect Hank from being punished, Kagan gave him a different prisoner number. To the nazis all Jews looked alike—we were no longer people. We had become numbers, and only by our numbers could we be distinguished. Unable to find the right number, they were unable to find Hank.

Throughout my days in the concentration camps I was fortunate to remain with my friend Mulya Atlas. We worked on the same shift and in the same area, lived in the same barracks, and shared the same bunk. Mulya was a big man, tall and strong, with an exuberant manner. A great raconteur, he would comment on a situation by telling a story that was supposed to make the point to the listener. If he felt the point had been missed, he would repeat the story and emphasize the punch line. Mulya would tell his stories with great expression and emotion, finish with a raucous, infectious laugh, slap the listener on the shoulder, and exclaim "Do you understand?" Sometimes Mulya and I would have public arguments, and our voices would rise into shouts. We were often referred to as the two *meshugoyim* (crazy ones). We enjoyed our arguments and would deliberately exaggerate them. In vain have I racked my brains trying to remember what we argued about because the arguments were not about anything per se but were argument for the sake of arguing, a welcome release of tension.

I loved Mulya dearly and relied on him for a great deal of emotional and practical support. As our situation worsened, our friendship grew stronger and closer. We would spend

Mulya and Dusya Atlas, New York, ca. 1958.

some evening hours squeezing blackheads from each other's faces. Without suitable lighting and mirrors, it was the only way to get rid of them. It was not about blackheads; it was the physical closeness we both craved. Mulya was not so much a father as an older brother to whom I listened and whom I admired. He was also much more than that: he was a true friend. To have a friend is a rare and valuable asset at any time. In the camps, where everyone was totally preoccupied with gaining even an infinitesimal advantage in ensuring their *own* survival, having such a friend was a treasure beyond value. I was very fortunate in having Mulya, and his presence was an important factor that helped me to survive the hardships of the camps.

Mulya had lost his wife and young child during the liquidation of the Large Ghetto. Like most other men in the camps, he did not talk about his family, and I never broached the subject. During our years together in the ghetto and the camps, Mulya never visited the Reichsjuden Ghetto, nor did he take up with another woman. After liberation Mulya immediately went back to Riga to look for his family, although with almost no hope of finding them. Only after confirming what he must have known already—that none of his family had survived—could he continue his life. In Riga he married Dusya, a young Jewish woman from Poland who had been with us in the camps. By obtaining documents stating they were Polish Jews, they managed to leave Soviet Latvia for Poland. From there they went to Berlin and on to the U.S. Zone of Occupation. In the early 1950s they were able to come to New York. Over the years, I kept in contact with him and visited him during my occasional trips to New York. In 1971 I took my oldest son, David, to meet him. I felt I was bringing his grandson for a visit.

Mulya died suddenly in 1977 of a ruptured aortic aneurism. My comrade-in-arms in our shared struggle for survival, Mulya represented an important link with the community from Riga. Losing him was a great shock, and I miss him greatly.

Despite the nazi efforts to degrade and dehumanize us, my friends and I never lost a sense of our humanity. Regardless of the humiliations and deprivations heaped on us by our jailers, there was never the slightest doubt that we were human, that we were the sane ones. It was the nazis who were monsters; they had created the demented world of the camps, they were the crazy ones. However difficult, in dealing with each other we tried to preserve a code of civilized conduct, retain our dignity, and respect the dignity of our fellow inmates. For the nazis, their collaborators, and all Germans, however, the rules of civilized behavior were suspended—any conduct was permissible, provided we could get away with it.

As the end of the war drew near, malnutrition and disease sapped me of my strength, and I found it increasingly difficult to maintain my composure. The beating had weakened me. It took weeks to recover, and I never regained my strength. For six months—ever since Kaiserwald—I had been on a starvation diet, and now my ankles were definitely swollen, a painful herald of my imminent collapse. I became lethargic and watched the days pass in a kind of daze. Nonetheless, buoyed by the certainty that any day now the war would be over, I never lost the drive for life; at critical moments a surge of energy pushed me to make whatever move seemed to offer the best chance of survival.

One of the strongest motivations that kept me going during the most difficult situations was the attraction and wonder of sex. I perceived my lack of sexual experience as a deprivation; I was determined to remain alive and someday acquire it. Even in my weakened condition, the anticipation of sex was a powerful impetus in my fight for survival.

Allied bombings were music to our ears—they promised liberation. It never occurred to me that we might be hit. It was a wonderful sound. In late February or March 1945 the tempo of the Allied air raids was stepped up, causing frequent work stoppages. Although the plant was not hit, it eventually stopped operating because of the loss of electrical power. Without the routine of daily work, the atmosphere in the camp became surreal. It felt as if we were in a kind of suspended animation. The war was very close around us. Yet here we were unable to do anything—we were still in the camp, still on a starvation diet, still under the cruel scourge of the nazis.

2 |

Liberation

Bis es kumt di nechome, geit arois di neshome.
The soul departs ere solace arrives.
—Yiddish proverb

Spring found me and my 500 fellow inmates still in the small slave labor camp at Polte-Werke at the outskirts of Magdeburg. We occasionally worked at clearing debris in the city but were mostly awaiting the imminent collapse of the Third Reich. On the morning of April 11, 1945, we unexpectedly found our camp unguarded. Four of us, led by my friend Mulya Atlas, immediately left the camp and set out toward the center of the city.

After a fifteen-minute walk we found ourselves surrounded by the ruins of what once had been a residential neighborhood. Allied bombing had gutted much of the city. Entire blocks had been reduced to burned-out shells. Only the stairwells, chimneys, and outer walls of the lower stories remained standing. There was no doubt that Germany had lost the war, but the sight of everything the Germans owned being reduced to a smoldering pile of ashes was a joy to behold.

We clambered over the piles of rubble and down into one of the cellars. All cellars were now connected, and one could move from building to building without having to go out on the street. We found frozen potatoes, which had baked in the embers when the buildings were on fire. We found some jars of preserves, which we ate with the unevenly baked potatoes. Having found some civilian clothes, we were in an exuberant mood. We had escaped and had only to wait for the Americans to arrive. We felt as if we were already liberated. On the next block we saw some shops in a small cluster of undamaged houses. I strutted into the neighborhood butcher shop and demanded meat. I promised to pay as soon as the Americans arrived. This did not impress the proprietor, and I left empty-handed. I nevertheless felt transformed. We were the victors, and I wanted to make sure the Germans knew it.

Our freedom had been made possible by an American armor column that had pushed toward Magdeburg. Anticipating the imminent fall of the city, our guards had fled during the night. But the U.S. advance halted just short of Magdeburg, and the city did not fall that day. The following day the SS guards returned to the Polte-Werke camp. The remaining inmates were taken on a death march to concentration camp Sachsenhausen. Some days later, because that camp was also in danger of being overrun by the Russians, the prisoners were driven on a further death march. Many were killed on the march.[49]

At night it grew bitterly cold, and after some time we decided to make a fire in a basement oven. We should have known better, but in our euphoria we did not think, and so our freedom was short-lived. Smoke from the chimney caught the attention of a German Volkssturm patrol—a local militia made up of old men and teenagers. Once again we were prisoners. Apparently, they were not quite sure what to do with us, so they marched us through town to a bridge crossing the Elbe River. At that point, no more eager than we were to cross the river, our escort told us to turn ourselves in on the other side, the eastern bank. We assured them that we would, and they returned to town. When we came off the first span of the bridge, we found ourselves on a small island. Flanking the road were attractive villas that had suffered only minor damage but nevertheless seemed abandoned. We selected one, entered the garage, and having barricaded the door with heavy boards, sat down to wait it out. We were certain the Americans and the end of the war could not be long in coming.

Over the next few days the war seemed to be coming closer: we could hear artillery, and there were explosions nearby. We continued to sit, waiting for the Americans and the end of the war. The Americans had indeed liberated Magdeburg and reached the River Elbe. By agreement with the Soviets their advance stopped at the Elbe, where they waited for the Soviet troops to meet up with them from the east. But the bridge connecting our island to Magdeburg had been bombed and destroyed. Although we did not know it, we were stranded in a no-man's-land between Allied and Russian lines.

The lull in the fighting weighed heavily on us. Days dragged into weeks. The world seemed to have passed us by; we had been forgotten. Our exhilaration at having escaped proved transitory, draining away into depression. I do not remember how we managed to get food, although I know we found some in the cellar of the villa. We also found a wonderful Rhine wine, but we shared only one bottle among us.

I was growing weaker by the day, and my diarrhea was getting worse. I was badly emaciated, and still I kept losing weight; I had ulcerated sores on my legs. Just beyond the backyard of our refuge was a small village where a German doctor had his office. Desperate, I decided to go see him. I made up a story about being a worker from the east, but he did not ask any questions. He examined me and put some ointment on my sores. There was no mention of a fee; I thanked him and made my way back to our hideout.

We waited. One of us would occasionally venture out to reconnoiter. One morning my friend came running back, shouting "the Red Army is here." Emerging from our garage, we soon met up with a Red Army patrol. We were told it was May 9 and Germany had surrendered the day before. The war was over. The soldiers were friendly but noncommittal. We were directed to a collection point 10 km down the road and were told to walk there. My friends argued that I needed immediate medical attention, that I could not possibly walk that distance, and that we must be taken by truck. It was to no avail. In the end we had to walk. My friends were furious with me for not demanding that we be driven. As they saw it I had selfishly failed to consider the common good. They went so far as to accuse me of having deprived them of their chance for survival. For myself, it was more a matter of not admitting that I was dying. I am convinced that my survival hinged on fighting for my life, on not giving in to or admitting my weakness.

At the collection point I was separated from my friends and was immediately taken to a Red Army field hospital. There must have been delousing, showers, a change of clothes, and similar activities, but I don't recall any details. All I remember is the Jewish woman doctor, a captain in the Red Army, who examined me and was kind and reassuring. Except for my fellow inmates, it was my first empathetic human encounter in many years. I had a feeling of profound relief: "I am free, I am among friends, my bed has clean linen, I can rest, I can let down my guard."

The field hospital was a typical Russian do-it-yourself institution. The less sick tended to the sicker patients. I was placed in the so-called intensive care unit, a small room with only four beds. A fellow patient assured me, "You will be dead by morning." I ignored his prediction. I knew I was safe.

22
Human Again

My recollections of the first months after liberation are hazy. For the first time in four years I could let down my guard. I felt cared for and was completely relaxed. After a few days in the military field hospital, I was transferred to a hospital for Soviet civilians where most of the patients were former slave laborers and concentration camp inmates. I spent several months in this hospital. Although the food was adequate, it was of poor quality: a lot of soup and potatoes and very little meat or protein. It was just as well. I was severely malnourished, and large amounts of rich food may have killed me. The ulcerated sores on my legs healed extremely slowly. The doctor was exasperated by my lack of progress and was particularly bothered by a persistent wound on my knee. To better promote healing she threatened to immobilize the knee by putting it in a cast. Regardless of whether the therapy was responsible, by July my condition had improved markedly.

Among the patients were several fellow inmates from the Polte camp. One was a dentist from Riga, Monya Zahl, with whom I became friendly. He was exploring the possibility of escaping to the western zones of occupation by way of Berlin. He even made a reconnaissance trip to Berlin and when he returned gave me detailed instructions on how to manage an escape. The hospital was soon to be closed, and all patients well enough to travel were being returned to their homes in the Soviet Union. Their departure was arranged on very short notice, and I did not have a chance to say good-bye to Monya. To my surprise, Monya decided to return to Riga.

By this time the prospect of returning to Riga no longer excited me. In the euphoria following liberation, I would have returned immediately had my health permitted it. The three months' period while I recuperated had given me pause to consider my future. I was certain my parents had been killed. The world I had known in Riga was gone, and Latvia appeared likely to remain under Soviet control. There was nothing for me there. Not just Latvia but all of Europe seemed like one vast cemetery, hardly a place in which to start a new life.

Of all the possibilities, the United States seemed the most attractive, but refugees seeking to go there needed an affidavit from someone living in the States pledging financial support. My uncle Leo was living in the United States, but I was not sure how to find him. So far as I knew, my aunts Clara and Thea were somewhere in the West. As it turned out, Thea was in Birmingham, England, but Clara was dead. She had been killed in Auschwitz after having been deported from Paris by the Vichy government.

I also seriously considered Palestine in spite of the fact that the British did not permit immigration there. Most survivors of the Holocaust had few choices; for them, Palestine was the only real option. Sooner or later Britain would have to yield to world pressure and open Palestine to the surviving Jews of Europe. Until then, for the younger people there was always *Aliyah Bet,* illegal immigration. Being penniless did not bother us. We assumed, and were later proven correct, that world Jewry would pick up the tab for our travel.

Although I did not yet know where I was going to go, I knew I did not want to go back to Latvia. Accordingly, I needed to delay my return to Riga long enough to set up and execute my escape. I decided that a transfer to a tuberculosis (TB) sanatorium would suit my purpose. It also offered a chance to get some better food and rest, which I still sorely needed. To set the stage for a diagnosis of TB, I started to complain of night sweats and chills. I was told to report to the nurse on three consecutive afternoons to have my temperature checked. The first two days I surreptitiously warmed up the thermometer by rubbing it against my wool sweater. On the third visit I was watched closely and did not have an opportunity to raise my temperature. Still, I may have had a slight fever, and the decision was made to transfer me to a German sanatorium.

It was a pleasant, quiet place, somewhat like the sanatorium in Thomas Mann's *Magic Mountain.* The food was good, and I spent a couple of restful weeks while the doctors took X rays and did a number of tests. Eventually they pronounced me well, ready to be discharged. I was sure I did not have TB, and the official confirmation did not thrill me. Far from being relieved, I was annoyed at having my planned recuperation cut short.

In late August I again found myself in a repatriation camp, the only Jew among a group of unhappy-looking Latvian refugees. They had only recently fled Latvia trying to escape the advancing Red Army. Now they were being forcibly repatriated to an uncertain future in their Soviet-occupied homeland. It was unfortunate for them, but I did not sympathize with them. The camp was quite primitive. We slept on two-level wooden bunks, men and women together. There were blankets but no mattresses, and the food, as in all Soviet camps, although provided in adequate quantities, was of poor quality.

I disliked my fellow inmates as much as I disliked the prospect of going back to Riga, but I was careful to keep this attitude to myself. On September 11, 1945, when it was announced that we were going to be shipped out, I was prepared to act: I told the camp manager I had left some personal possessions in town and was eager to take them with me on my return to the "beloved homeland." He let me go into town and instructed me to join the convoy on my way back. Once out of the camp I never looked back. A civilian train took me straight to Berlin, where I arrived by midafternoon. I traveled light. I literally had nothing other than the clothes on my back. I was wearing an old blue German air force jacket I had managed to appropriate. I was no longer emaciated, and although shabby and threadbare, I did not look out of place in the surging crowds of tattered refugees.

Monya had given me the address of the Jewish Community Office in Berlin. They would help me make all necessary arrangements for continuing my travels to the West. I took the U-Bahn (the Berlin subway) to the indicated stop, which turned out to be a neighborhood located in the Soviet sector of the city. I had trouble finding the place. I finally did, only to discover that the building had been bombed and destroyed. There was no time to inquire. It was getting dark, and I was still in the Soviet sector. I was afraid to remain there overnight. I took the subway to the first stop in the American sector, located the nearest German city police station, and went inside. I explained that I was a German Jew from Cologne released from KZ Buchenwald and was on my way back home in search of my relatives. I had been referred to the Jewish community but had not been able to find the office, and I asked permission to stay overnight in their lockup. At the time, former residents of Eastern Europe were being forcibly repatriated, and I was determined to pass as a Jew from western Germany. Cologne was the first German city in the West that came to mind, and I decided it may as well become my new birthplace. Despite my obvious Baltic German accent, there were no awkward questions.

Although tense and anxious, I spent a relatively restful night in the lockup. My demands were modest, and I found the accommodations excellent. Early the next morning my hosts offered me a cup of coffee and some rolls, and I was again on my way. It was very curious. A few months earlier the police were my sworn enemy, to be avoided at all costs. Now they were helping me escape to the West.

I resumed my search for the elusive Jewish Community Office. This time my efforts were rewarded. I found the office just two houses beyond the spot where I had been the day before. I was given a friendly reception. I repeated my story of being a Jew from Cologne, saying I wanted to return

·Jüdische Gemeinde zu Berlin

Berlin N 4, den 12.9.1945
Oranienburger Str. 28
Tel.: 42 33 28

Betr.: Ne/Sz

B e s c h e i n i g u n g

Wir bescheinigen hiermit Herrn Max M i c h e l s o h n, geb.2.10.24
daß er Jude ist und jetzt aus dem Konzentrationslager Buchenwald
entlassen worden ist.
Wir bitten alle Militär- und Zivilbehörden, ihm jede Unterstützung
zu gewähren. Sein Reiseziel ist nach Frankfurt/Main zu seinen
Angehörigen.

Jüdische Gemeinde
zu Berlin

Certificate issued to me by the Jewish Community Office in Berlin.

there and also to search for my relatives in the United States and England.
It was suggested that Frankfurt/Main, in the American Zone of Occupation, was a more appropriate destination. I was furnished with a certificate
requesting that both military and civilian authorities assist me in my travels. The document stated that I was a Jew released from KZ Buchenwald,
now on my way to Frankfurt in search of relatives. It was the first identification document I had received since my liberation. It was a wonderful
feeling to recover my name and no longer be just a number. I also was
greatly relieved that I no longer had to worry about falling into Soviet
hands. I was told to report to a United Nations Relief and Rehabilitation
Administration (UNRRA) camp for displaced persons (DPs) in Zehlendorf
(in the American sector of Berlin), where I would find transport to western
Germany.

That day, September 12, 1945, while at the Jewish Community Office
in Berlin, I initiated a search for Leo in New York and Thea in Birmingham. I do not remember sending a notice to Clara in Paris. France had
been occupied by the Germans, and I was not sure about Clara's whereabouts. Although I did not think she had been killed, I had no idea where
to look for her. As it happened, my message reached Thea and Arthur in
Birmingham, and they immediately notified Leo. It was the first news about
our family in Riga they had received since the German attack on Russia
more than four years earlier. Both Leo and Arthur wrote to me in care of
the Jewish community in Berlin, but the letters never reached me. I also

failed to receive several packages Leo sent to Berlin because I had already moved on to Frankfurt. Mail service to Germany was still erratic, and it took several months to establish direct communications.

Long after Arthur's and Thea's deaths, I found a copy of Arthur's letter to me among his papers. On October 19, 1945, Arthur had written to the Home Office requesting permission for me to enter the United Kingdom and offering to guarantee my maintenance. The official response, dated December 5, expressed regrets that "the Secretary of State . . . is unable to assist" because only males under eighteen were eligible for admission to the United Kingdom. I was not aware of Arthur's initiative, as neither he nor Thea ever mentioned it. Considering Arthur's difficult financial position, his prompt attempt to help me and his offer of support were truly generous. I regret not having been able to thank him.

After a fortnight in the Zehlendorf UNRRA camp, we were taken by semitrailer to Braunschweig in the British zone. Here I met a former campmate from Riga and Polte, Leonid Pancis. There was strong camaraderie among our community of survivors, a bond of shared ordeals and the joy of deliverance. We knew who lived where and could depend on a warm welcome whenever one of us suddenly turned up on the doorstep. Pancis had recently married Lilly, a German Jewish girl who had been deported to Riga and whom he had met in the Riga Ghetto. Lilly had survived Stutthof, and Leonid and Lilly had again happily found each other.[50] They were settled comfortably in Braunschweig, and I spent a couple of days with them. Then I took a civilian train to Frankfurt, a ten-hour ride in an overcrowded, standing-room-only railroad car. Arriving in Frankfurt utterly exhausted, I reported to the DP camp Zeilsheim at the outskirts of the city where I was warmly greeted by a number of survivors from Riga.

Since the camp facilities were primitive and crowded, my friends had rented rooms or apartments in the small village of Zeilsheim, adjacent to the DP camp. They had been here for several months and were able to advise me as to where to find work and where to live. With their help I soon found a job in a U.S. Army mess hall in Frankfurt. My friend Sam Donde and I rented a room in the city and moved out of the DP camp. We shared the master bedroom in the apartment of an elderly German couple, who gave up their bedroom and slept in the parlor. We had kitchen privileges for some light cooking. Our landlords were a working-class couple who needed the money. Although they were pleasant and polite, we never became friendly.

Retaining my "camp mentality," I viewed the army mess hall as an ideal place to work: it was near a kitchen. Shortly after starting work at the mess hall, in early December 1945, I was caught stealing 3 pounds of sugar. I did not need the sugar, nor did I intend to sell it. I was just obsessed with food. For me, there was never enough food. I would take whatever was available. Although I now lived in free-dom, the mind-set conditioned by sla-very and the camps persisted. Ac-quired over years of deprivation and hunger, this behavior persisted long after the war was over. My friends also routinely pilfered food. I had not accepted the responsibility for my actions that goes with freedom. I had to learn that the rules of freedom are not the rules of the camps or slavery. It was the most painful episode in my return to normal, civilian life.

After spending the night in the army lockup, I appeared next morn-ing before a U.S. Army captain in summary administrative proceedings. Viewing all Germans as nazis, I promptly got into a tiff with the young German woman serving as his inter-preter. "I can speak English," I de-clared haughtily. "I don't need an in-terpreter." What I meant but did not

My first formal photo after the war, Frankfurt, 1946. I am wearing the blue DP uniform.

say was that I would not allow myself to be represented by a German inter-preter. Despite my insistence, my English was hardly adequate, and refus-ing the interpreter did not help my case. It took only a few minutes: the judge made some remarks about having to fight the prevalent pilfering and sentenced me to two weeks in the city jail. It is instructive to contrast the American and nazi legal systems. In the camps my offense would have resulted in immediate execution.

In jail I had ample time to contemplate the errors of my ways. Because of my short sentence, the authorities did not consider it worthwhile to assign me work. I spent most of the two weeks in solitary confinement. It may have been a short sentence, but the hours seemed to pass at a snail's pace. It was a very bitter lesson. I painfully recalled my friend and mentor Victor Kron and his exacting ethical standards and uncompromising views on stealing. When finally I was released, I returned to the apartment chas-tened by the experience.

In February 1946 I found a good job as an English-Polish interpreter in the mess hall of a U.S. Army Medical General Dispensary. I helped the American supervisors communicate with the mess hall workers, a group of Polish DPs. My English was fair, my Polish poor; nonetheless, I managed to translate well enough so the Poles and Americans could communicate.

My only noteworthy failure occurred when I had to instruct a Polish worker to clean the toilet. He did not understand until I took him by the hand and showed him what was wanted. In the process I learned (and have never forgotten) the Polish word for toilet: *ustemp.* I was given the blue U.S. Army–style uniform worn by the DP workers, but my civilian wardrobe was extremely limited. I had managed to get some pants and a presentable jacket, but I did not feel properly dressed. When going to the theater or a nightclub I wanted to dress up, but I did not own a suit, and black market prices were way beyond my means. We were paid in army scrip, which was adequate to cover my daily needs but did not permit me to purchase anything extra. For three cartons of cigarettes (the standard of exchange), which I was able to obtain relatively easily, I bought a gold wristwatch, but I did not own a suit until after arriving in New York. As DPs we did not enjoy Post Exchange (PX) privileges. We were allowed to attend the U.S. Army cinema, however, and I spent many evenings watching the latest American movies. Among many others, I saw David Niven in *Stairway to Heaven,* Fred Astaire in *Stork Club,* and *Road to Utopia* with Bing Crosby. I was particularly impressed by Rita Hayworth in *Gilda.* The films, screened without subtitles, helped improve my English considerably.

While in Frankfurt I established contact with my uncle Michel and my aunt Nyura Griliches in Paris. I received several letters and a package from them, and they informed Leo of my whereabouts. They also sent me Leo's correct address so I could finally contact him directly. About the same time, the former daughter-in-law of Jakob Kaplan, Helene (Linika) Kaplan, then a physician in the Free French Forces, came on an official visit to Frankfurt. She got in touch with me and delivered greetings from Leo. Although I had never met her before, I had heard a lot about her and was delighted to find another relative. We spent a pleasant afternoon together.

Now that I was in touch with Leo, I definitely decided to go to the United States. I knew Leo well and felt close to him. Reuniting with one of the few surviving members of my family was a priority. It seemed an auspicious way to begin mending my interrupted life. Leo started the process to get me a U.S. visa. Although there was little question that I would eventually receive my visa, the quota for Latvian-born immigrants was small, and the wait for a visa was correspondingly long.*

In spring of 1946, on one of my periodic visits to Zeilsheim, I met Manya, a young woman from Riga. She had spent the war years in the Soviet Union and had only recently escaped to the West. She now lived in

---

*The total number of immigrants admitted to the United States from the European portion of the USSR, Finland, and the Baltic states was 153 in 1946 and 761 in 1947.

Zeilsheim, where she rented a small apartment outside the DP camp and worked at a school for the children in the camp. Manya was a determined young woman who resolutely pursued her goals. An ardent Zionist, she viewed her stay in Frankfurt as temporary. She had left the Soviet Union expecting to go to Palestine. Even though *Aliyah Bet* was the only route available, she expected to get there in the near future. Getting into Palestine had proved more difficult than she had imagined, however, and the prospect of spending years waiting in Germany was repugnant to her. During the summer, as my plans for emigration solidified, Manya also began to think about going to the United States, but without a sponsor to provide an affidavit of support, that was not possible.

After receiving my U.S. visa in September 1946, I quit my job at the U.S. Army mess hall. I received a good recommendation from my captain. My immediate supervisor, the mess sergeant, presented me with his silver pocket watch as a keepsake. We had become friendly, and he had helped correct and improve my English. He repeatedly admonished me not to say "what, what" but rather "excuse me; would you please repeat that." Although I do not recall his name I treasure the watch, which is still running.

My departure was delayed by a shipping strike in the United States. Manya now talked of marriage and of joining me in the United States. For me, the prospect of marriage seemed premature; I had not even finished high school. My single-minded goal was to rebuild my interrupted life, and as much as I liked Manya, I was not ready for marriage. After I left Frankfurt, Manya and I corresponded frequently. Late in 1947 Manya wrote that she had married a young man from Poland. After lengthy delays, they were also able to come to the United States.

With three friends from Riga—Alex Kahn, Joseph Kussman, and Uri Joffe—all fellow survivors of the nazi camps, I spent eight weeks in a resettlement camp near Frankfurt awaiting the end of the shipping strike. In November we traveled to Bremerhaven where we spent seven more weeks waiting for a ship to take us to the New World. Finally, in early January 1947, we embarked on the U.S.S. *Ernie Pyle,* a Liberty ship troop carrier. My material possessions fit comfortably into one small suitcase. I left Europe without any regrets; it held bitter memories of death and destruction. The United States was not just the land of opportunity; to me it represented a new beginning, the promise of a new life, as well as the prospect of reuniting with Uncle Leo and a chance for a normal existence. After a stormy twelve-day voyage, I arrived in New York.

23
Finding Relatives

As soon as the war in Europe ended, survivors started searching frantically for their lost relatives and friends. Lists of survivors from different towns were posted in Jewish displaced persons camps, and stories as to who had been seen and where they were headed circulated widely by word of mouth. Everybody was on the move: back to their native cities and towns or away toward the West or to Israel. Most survivors were soon in touch with each other. Only the dead were not heard from, and unfortunately there were all too many of them. People caught in the Soviet Union took longer to surface. In the initial confusion after the war, some managed to reach the West through Poland, but many did not get out until the 1970s, when emigration of Jews to Israel and the United States again became possible.

In Frankfurt I found and made contact with my cousin Zvi Griliches. His family (Uncle Fima and Aunt Clara Griliches, Zvi, and his younger sister Ellen) had lived in Kaunas (Kovno) when Germany overran Lithuania.

In Kaunas the liquidation of the ghetto and the destruction of the Jewish community had been less precipitous, although no less ruthless or efficient, than in Riga. By 1943 there was no mistaking the nazis' intentions. Determined to save her nine-year-old daughter, Ellen, Clara arranged to spirit her out of the ghetto and managed to get Ellen into a Lithuanian Catholic orphanage. Ellen remained successfully hidden until liberation. Clara was not so lucky. When the ghetto was liquidated in June 1944, Clara, together with her husband and son, was deported to Stutthof, where the men and women were separated. Clara died there of typhoid fever. Fima and Zvi were sent to a small camp near Munich, part of the Dachau system of camps. Weakened by malnutrition and dysentery, Fima died there in January 1945. He was buried, in Zvi's presence, in a cemetery near the camp where a small number of other prisoners were also buried. Unlike most victims of the Holocaust, his grave site is known. After the

Fima and Clara Zvi Griliches, ca. 1936.

war Zvi returned and placed a monument on the grave where, to the best of his recollection, his father had been buried.

Shortly after liberation Ellen recounted these events in a Yiddish news-letter published in Munich:

> Once on a winter night Mama and Papa took me to the [ghetto] gate.
> There stood a car, and the Jewish police ordered us to push the car.
> While they were pushing the car, I walked out of the Ghetto with my
> Mama. A Christian boy waited for me there. He led me away to his
> place, an apartment in a street near Sabar. I stayed there for two days.
> While I was with the Christian, my Mama came for me and took me to
> the Kovno Christian Children's home. I stayed there two or three days.
> They were told that I was a Russian child, because I spoke Russian well.
> Then a peasant came and took me away to a village Tamoshava, near
> Aukshte Dveris, to a children's home. There I worked with all the
> children, peeled potatoes, worked in the fields. The children did not
> know that I was a Jewish child. However, the adults there knew that I
> was a Jewish child. There were also Jewish girls, younger than I. I could
> recognize that from their faces. They did not know that I was a Jewish
> child, and one did not speak about it.
>
> When the Russians came back, I still remained at the children's home.
> My mother and father were deported to Germany together with all the

Ellen, 1949, and Zvi, 1948.

Jews from the ghetto. But one of my aunts, Leah Olitzki, escaped from the columns when the Jews were led from the ghetto to the station. After the Russians came to Kovno, my aunt asked a Jewish acquaintance, Levin, who then lived near the children's home, to pick me up. His sisters came to get me. I lived with them for three weeks; then they brought me to Kovno.

When the war ended, Jews from the KZs came back to Kovno. I learned from them that my father had died in KZ Dachau, and my Mama died in KZ Stutthof. My brother survived Dachau.[51]

Just before the end of the war, Zvi was returned to the main camp at Dachau. From there he was taken on a death march into the mountains of Bavaria. As Allied armies threatened to overrun a concentration camp, the SS guards evacuated the inmates on forced marches away from the front lines and toward the interior of Germany. Conditions on death marches were particularly brutal, and inmates who fell behind were executed on the spot. Zvi was ultimately liberated by the U.S. Army. After liberation he went to Munich and soon met up with his mother Clara's younger brother, his uncle Solly Griliches, also a survivor of Stutthof and Dachau. In spring of 1946 Zvi visited me in Frankfurt, where we had a bittersweet reunion. The little boy I remembered was now a tall, self-reliant young man. I was overjoyed to see him, but at the same time it was a painful reminder of the families we both had lost.

During the liquidation of the Kaunas Ghetto and the evacuation of its inmates to Stutthof, Clara's sister-in-law Leah Olitzki managed to escape. She remained hidden in Kaunas until she was liberated by the Red Army. Leah then retrieved Ellen and Solly's two children, eight-year-old Henry-Imma and three-year-old Ilana, who had also been hidden in Lithuanian orphanages, and took them to Kaunas. When the war ended, Leah escaped with them to Berlin. Solly, whose wife was also killed in Stutthof, had been liberated near Munich. With the help of an American soldier, he met his sister-in-law in Berlin and brought them all to Munich where he was living with Bella, also a survivor. He took Ellen and Zvi into his new household.

Zvi stayed with Solly in Munich for about a year. Then he joined a group of young orphaned survivors who in February 1947 made *Aliyah,* the return to the Jewish homeland. Immigration to Palestine was illegal. Their ship was intercepted by the British, and they were interned on Cyprus for six months. In September 1947 Britain admitted the children into Palestine, and Youth Aliyah (a branch of the Zionist movement that rescued orphans and children separated from their parents and resettled them in Israel) settled Zvi on a kibbutz. After World War II, Youth Aliyah brought about 15,000 child survivors of the Holocaust to kibbutzim, or children's villages, in Israel.

Solly had also intended to go to Palestine but now changed his plans. In 1949 he took the children to the United States and settled in New York. Solly married Bella, and Ellen continued to live in their household.

Uncle Michel and Aunt Nyura Griliches, who lived in Paris, had escaped to unoccupied France and had survived the war there. By 1945 they were back in their Paris apartment. When their fourteen-year-old nephew Zvi and twelve-year-old niece Ellen emerged from the camps, Michel and Nyura did not open their home to them. Ellen, to be sure, was provided for; she went with her uncle Solly to New York. Solly had two small children of his own, and taking responsibility for Ellen was an added hardship for him. I received several nice letters from Nyura, but we did not continue to keep in touch. She had forwarded my letter to Leo and knew he would arrange for my emigration to the United States.

I found Michel's attitude incomprehensible. I saw nothing to prevent Michel and Nyura from bringing their underage nephew Zvi to Paris. But even after the horrendous catastrophe that had befallen us all, he was unwilling to reach out to the victims. What resentment could Michel possibly harbor that would prevent him from taking in his own brother's orphaned children? In my old age I have come to take a more charitable view. I now regard Michel as an ineffectual and pathetic person. He may have felt overwhelmed and thought he would be unable to cope with two teenage children.

Zvi remembered our uncle Boris's address in Moscow, which his father, Fima, had impressed upon him. After liberation Zvi wrote to him from Munich. The letter reached Boris, who immediately sent Zvi a telegram and then a letter. Zvi never met Boris, who died in the early 1950s. When Zvi was able to visit Moscow in the 1960s, he met Boris's widow, Anna, who gave us pictures of our grandfather and the uncles who had lived in the Soviet Union.

My cousins Ellen and Zvi and I were the only survivors of all our relatives caught in German-occupied Eastern Europe. My cousin Mako Michelson and uncle Artur Keilman were shipped from Kaiserwald to Stutthof in August 1944 on an earlier transport than I. Both were then transferred to Buchenwald. Keilman must have died there, but Mako was liberated by the U.S. Army on April 11, 1945. My uncle Leo thought he recognized Mako in a photo of emaciated prisoners taken in Buchenwald shortly after liberation. Although Mako's name appears on a list of survivors published in 1946 in Munich, he did not surface after the war. Upon my recent inquiry I received notice from the International Tracing Service that Mako died of pulmonary tuberculosis two months after liberation. Unfortunately, I have been unable to locate his grave site.

I lost track of my cousin Paul Dawidson in Riga when I was sent to Kaiserwald. As there is no record of him at Stutthof, he was probably killed in Kaiserwald or at another camp in Latvia.

24
A New Country, a New Beginning

In New York Leo greeted me at the dock and took me to his studio apartment at 58 West 57th Street, where I was installed on a couch in the foyer. Leo and Jennie Tourel had separated and now had their own apartments, although they continued to care deeply for each other and maintained a lifelong friendship. They simply could not live together. Leo confided that living with a temperamental artist had become too difficult. Leo could also be difficult to live with. He would, in a disarmingly charming manner and without explicitly raising any objection, stubbornly persist in doing exactly as he pleased.

Leo shared his studio with Minos, his miniature French poodle, who had escaped the Germans together with Leo and Jennie. Minos was a lovely, highly intelligent dog but was given to jealousy when people came to visit. If he felt neglected he communicated his displeasure by chewing a finger off any gloves the unwary visitor may have left in the entryway. When it was time to leave, Leo's guests would discover the mutilation, and an embarrassed Leo would try to make restitution. Consequently, Leo bought many pairs of new gloves. In fact, Minos honored me at our first meeting by venting his spleen on my precious pair of leather gloves, which I had unsuspectingly left on the table.

I quickly got used to life in New York; in fact, I loved being there. Leo and I adapted well to living together and settled into a comfortable bachelor existence. I helped in the apartment and ran errands for him. We did not cook much but ate a lot of delicatessen cold cuts. Leo was obviously happy to have brought me over and proudly introduced me to his friends. Some of them perceived a family resemblance between us and often asked whether I was Leo's son. During summer 1947 Leo went to Europe for an extended visit, and I looked after Minos and his stateside affairs. My English was adequate for face-to-face situations, but I found telephone conversations difficult.

To make up for years lost in the camps, I was determined to finish my schooling as quickly as possible. My intent was to become an electronics engineer, an ambition I had nursed since before the war. In my mind there was no question that I would achieve this goal. Ten days after landing in New York I started attending the YMCA Evening High School just three blocks from Leo's studio. I enrolled in fourth-year English, advanced algebra, and solid geometry, subjects I had not previously studied. My English was still somewhat shaky, but I had little difficulty keeping up with my classes.

Despite the six-year interruption, I adjusted easily to the school routine. In fact, after years of manual labor I found the world of ideas extremely stimulating. I was unfamiliar with modern American literature and began to read voraciously. In addition to the required reading for school, I became acquainted with the influential contemporary American authors of the time: Theodore Dreiser, John Dos Passos, Sinclair Lewis, Richard Wright, and others. Most of my classmates were also in their early or mid-twenties, and I felt comfortable there. After completing the spring term I took several Regents tests, the New York statewide high school examinations. Having attended high school in Riga, I essentially picked up where I had left off in 1941. I was permitted to take Regents even in subjects I had not studied here. Upon completing a second term of fourth-year English, chemistry, and trigonometry during the summer semester, I passed more Regents and received my high school diploma.

The next step was college. A friend suggested exploring the possibility of entering the Massachusetts Institute of Technology. We took a bus to Cambridge, Massachusetts, for an interview with the admissions officer. He listened sympathetically to my story, and upon learning of my lack of financial resources, he advised me that the City College of New York (CCNY) was an excellent school and that I should plan to attend it. Following his advice, I applied and was admitted to CCNY as an evening student in an electrical engineering course. CCNY was free, but as I did not meet the one-year city residency requirement I had to pay a modest $110 tuition for my first term. In February 1948, having fulfilled the residency requirement and satisfactorily completed my first-term courses, I was admitted as a full-time day student. As in high school, my fellow students at CCNY were generally older. Many were returning veterans studying under the GI Bill of Rights who were also anxious to complete their education as rapidly as possible.

So I would not be totally dependent on Leo for support, I sought full-time employment while I attended school. I worked a succession of temporary, low-paying unskilled jobs. I worked on an assembly line in a transformer factory, for a company that contracted to clean ships, as a night clerk in a maintenance company for neon advertising signs, and as a busboy in a cafeteria. The transformer factory was a union shop, so I joined the Electrical and Communications Workers Union. Union scale was a dollar an hour, a relatively good wage for unskilled work. Unfortunately, the factory ran out of orders, and after one month I was laid off. I got my next job from one of Leo's friends who owned a company that contracted the cleaning of passenger and troop ships. The day's work assignments were handed out at a "shape up" every morning at six o'clock at the union hall. During the first week I worked just one day, and with no prospect of more steady employment I quit after one week.

My next position was as a night clerk for a company that repaired neon signs. I prepared work orders for the maintenance people for the following day. I was familiar with night shift work, having done it in the camps, and did not anticipate that I would find it so exhausting. After attending evening classes I would take the subway to work. The early morning hours, about 3:00 to 6:00 A.M., were the most difficult. At 7:00 I would take the subway home, sleep until early afternoon, and then get up to do my homework. Jennie Tourel's apartment was near my school, and she kindly offered me her place so I could sleep undisturbed. That helped some, but after three weeks I was delighted when I was recalled to the transformer factory. It was a relief to get off the night shift.

I could manage working full-time jobs while I was in high school, but after starting college in fall of 1947 I looked for part-time positions. During my four years at CCNY I was first a counterman during the rush hours at a luncheonette in midtown Manhattan and later a lab assistant at Sintercast, a metallurgical research laboratory. CCNY offered afternoon and evening courses to accommodate working students, and I was able to arrange a convenient schedule with early morning and late afternoon or evening classes. I could work thirty hours per week while carrying a full course load. I worked at Sintercast for about three and a half years and was eventually promoted to junior metallurgist.

In spring of 1947 I became acquainted with Julia Brooks, a beautiful, spirited young woman. We first met on a double date. My date was Leah, and Julie was the blind date of my friend George. I had met Leah, a young woman who was also from Riga, through some friends of Leo's. Leah had a very nice girlfriend and thought it would be enjoyable for all of us to go out together. We met Julie at Leah's apartment and decided to go to a movie. After the movie we all decided to take Julie home together. Julie lived in Forest Hills, and we did not want her to take the long subway ride alone. The three of us lived in Manhattan, so it would not be a lonely ride back to the city. At Julie's house we were greeted by her parents, who then discreetly withdrew to their room. Julie served coffee and pastry, and we settled comfortably in the living room. We had an animated discussion about the movie we had just seen and other current topics. The evening left me with a lasting impression of Julie as a charming, intelligent, and very personable young woman. I felt very attracted to her.

Several months later we met again at a party. As before, we each had our own date. Believing it auspicious that fate had once again brought us together, I decided to pursue our friendship. I asked her out, but Julie said no. Nevertheless, six months and various complications later, she assented. In early summer 1948 we began to see each other regularly.

I proposed to Julie in August 1948. I was still living in Leo's studio apartment at the time. Leo was spending the summer in Paris as usual. In keeping with family tradition, I neglected to write to him about Julie or that I was planning to get married. Meanwhile, in Paris Leo had been courting a young French-woman, Janine Arnoud, and they were planning to marry. She was going to join him in New York shortly thereafter, and my continued presence in his apartment was impractical. Leo was uncomfortable about asking me to leave and put off informing me of his plans for as long as possible, so I had no inkling of this. When Leo returned to New York that fall, I reluctantly told him about my plans to move. Leo, of course, took the news well. Thus, much to our mutual relief, we discovered a happy coincidence of intentions as far as living arrangements were concerned.

Julie Brooks, 1948.

Julie and I were married in December 1948. We rented a one-room apartment on the Upper West Side of Manhattan. My friends at CCNY teased me: they observed that I no longer hung around after my evening classes but immediately departed for home.

Janine joined Leo in early 1949. She was a charming woman, very French, and Julie and I were delighted to make her acquaintance. Leo was eager to show her the sights of New York. We once met them just as they were returning from Rockefeller Center. Leo had expected her to be over-whelmed by the sights and thought it had been magnificent—"magnifique." Janine was not overwhelmed and allowed only that it was "grand." An argument ensued in French over whether the center really was magnificent or simply big, with neither of them about to concede the point. Janine was the

Leo and Janine, ca. 1965.

quintessential Frenchwoman: always chic and having definite opinions. For her, the innate superiority of everything French was axiomatic.

Leo and Janine spent their summers in Europe, mostly in Paris, but by autumn they were always back in New York. Leo's apartment consisted of just the big studio, a tiny kitchen, and the entrance foyer that had served as my room. The studio, which also served as Leo and Janine's bedroom, provided no privacy for Janine. If Leo had visitors or was working in the studio, Janine had nowhere to go. Leo moved to a larger apartment, also on West 57th Street, that in addition to a studio had separate living quarters. Janine settled comfortably into the New York scene and made many close friends.

When Leo died in 1978, Janine asked me to arrange the funeral. She preferred a traditional religious service, and through the funeral home I selected a conservative rabbi to officiate. I had overlooked the fact that Leo had wanted to be cremated, which is not accepted in Jewish religious practice.

In discussing the service with the rabbi I indicated that I would say the mourner's Kaddish, whereas he insisted that there was no burial and the Kaddish, usually recited at the grave, could not be said. To me it was of utmost importance that the full religious ceremony be performed. The hurried, haphazard burials I had witnessed during the Holocaust were still foremost in my mind, and I was determined that Leo's funeral would be a solemn religious occasion. Accordingly, I made it plain to the rabbi that no matter what, I was going to recite the Kaddish. He reluctantly agreed. When the time came we recited the Kaddish together, albeit at breakneck speed. Leo's friend, the violinist Tossy Spivakovsky, played two Bach sonatas, and another friend chanted the El Male Rachamim. It was a dignified event and a respectful ending to Leo's life. While grieving the loss of Leo, I was profoundly grateful that I was in a position to make the necessary arrangements to honor his memory.

After Leo's death Janine strove tirelessly to find a suitable home for his paintings. She ultimately succeeded in establishing the Michelson Museum of Art in Marshall, Texas, as a permanent showplace for Leo's art. Janine's love for and devotion to Leo both during and after his lifetime have been clearly evident. In April 1992 Janine died peacefully in Marshall, knowing she had accomplished her aim of securing Leo's heritage. She was a close and dear member of our family.

25

Building a Life

When Julie and I married, she was a social worker with the Department of Public Welfare. Later she worked as probation officer for the Domestic Relations Court. We were able to live quite comfortably on her salary, supplemented by my earnings from the laboratory job. Upon my graduation from CCNY in spring of 1951, Sintercast, my employer the previous three years, offered me a permanent position as a metallurgical engineer. Having no formal training in metallurgy, I felt inadequately prepared. Metallurgy seemed an art, whereas electronics, a more exact science, held more appeal for me. I had trained long and hard to be an electrical engineer, and I wanted to be one. When Raytheon Company offered me a position in Massachusetts, I accepted, and Julie and I moved to the relative wilds of the Boston area.

After I emerged from nazi hell, I was inclined to distance myself from my wartime experiences and concentrate on rebuilding my life. I tried to avoid recalling the painful events of the recent past. Except for occasionally reminiscing with fellow survivors, I rarely spoke about the war years, and then only in general terms. In my effort to forget the horrors I was abetted by New York Jewish society, which for its own reasons was not eager to hear about the nazi atrocities and murders. Through Leo I met a number of people who were active in the Jewish community. It was not uncommon for someone to express an interest in my experiences, saying "sometime you must tell me all about them." But the conversations never took place.

An exception was the philosopher and prominent American Zionist Horace Kallen, who queried me searchingly about life in the ghettos and camps. I told him about the persecutions and described my experiences at some length, although without going into the painful details. He did not press me. He seemed to sense my hesitation and refrained from asking intrusive questions. For me, the pain and anguish associated with the camp experiences were still too raw.

It is said that some survivors feel guilty over being the only ones in their families to have lived through the Holocaust. I have not found that to be the case among my fellow survivors. Occasionally, I have been asked whether I share this sense of guilt. My survival was a happenstance, an improbable chance occurrence, but I did not survive at the expense of anyone else, and I do not feel any guilt about it.

Julie has reminded me that soon after our marriage I spent an entire night giving her a lengthy account of my life during the war years. Julie was an attentive and sensitive listener, and it encouraged me to relate to my new bride the important events of my life. I believe it established a trust and a closer relationship between us.

I associated Judaism with rigid Orthodoxy, and although I identified strongly with being Jewish, it was in a secular and cultural rather than a religious sense. Before the war I had resented Agudat Israel's anti-Zionist policies and its efforts to enforce orthodox religious observance. In the camps the more observant sometimes used religious scruples to shirk unpleasant assignments, which they then tried to foist onto the nonobservant fellows. A particularly difficult situation occurred when we were forced to bury the people killed during the evacuation of the Large Ghetto. Several men in our group claimed to be *kohanim,* descended from the priestly class and by Jewish law prohibited from touching a corpse. Under normal circumstances we would have observed their religious principles. But this was not a normal time, and we felt our orthodox coworkers used the prohibition as a pretext to avoid disagreeable and strenuous tasks.

Although antireligious, I was intensely interested in the progress made toward achieving a Jewish state. I avidly followed the latest developments. After the Holocaust an independent Jewish state in Palestine was the only viable solution for the survivors of Eastern European Jewry. The establishment of Israel in 1948 was the emotional high point of Jewish life in the early postwar years. Having survived the worst catastrophe to befall the Jewish people since the destruction of the Second Temple, it was a unique privilege for me to witness the rebirth of a Jewish state, a sovereign Israel, after 2,000 years of exile.

After our sons were born, I wanted to pass on to them my sense of Jewish identity and heritage. I took adult education courses and became more involved in Judaism. To accommodate Julie's lack of knowledge of Hebrew, we joined a Reform synagogue. Religion is an important aspect of our lives, and over the years I have become more observant. I am a regular member of the Shabbat morning minyan at our synagogue. Judaism has always encompassed a wide diversity of practices. The fundamentalist right must not be allowed to be the only arbiters of those practices. Contrary to the current nostalgic and romanticized view, shtetl life was also characterized by ignorance, squalor, and the tyranny of a fossilized Orthodoxy.

Ellen and Zvi, 1992. Courtesy, Jane Akiba.

During the frightful days leading up to the Six-Day War, I was painfully reminded of my strong emotional ties to the State of Israel. The threat of another Holocaust at the hands of the Arabs loomed as a distinct and terrifying possibility. Israel's lightning victory seemed like a miracle and brought an emotional release of my tension and anxiety. It was a wonderful feeling, almost a second liberation. It also made me conscious of my commitment to the survival and well-being of Israel and the Jewish people. With Julie's wholehearted support I became involved in Jewish communal organizations. I was active in the Greater Framingham Jewish Federation. Julie and I were cofounders and later successive presidents of Jewish Family Service of Metrowest. The growth of our Jewish community has given me great satisfaction and a sense of accomplishment.

It wasn't until twenty-five years had elapsed that I gained distance from the wartime events and was able to speak publicly about my experiences in the camps and the incidents I witnessed. I believe my talks give meaning to my survival and that by recalling the persecutions I honor my family, friends, acquaintances, and fellow inmates who did not survive. Furthermore, as a survivor I have an obligation to bear witness to the horrors of the Holocaust, particularly in light of the lies spread by revisionist historians who are denying that the Holocaust occurred. I am a resource speaker with Facing History and Ourselves, an organization based in Boston, and am frequently called upon to speak about my wartime experiences in schools, churches, and synagogues. It is gratifying to interact with young audiences who are truly interested in learning about the persecutions. I believe that by speaking I am fighting prejudice, anti-Semitism, and racism.

I worked for Raytheon until my retirement in 1990 and have lived in the same house (with some additions) for more than forty years. Framingham is our home, and Julie and I have no plans to move. We have, of course, had our share of life's vicissitudes and problems. We have faced them together, and our marriage has been a happy one. Our sons have grown into fine young men, and we have three delightful grandchildren: Rebecca, Daniel, and Anna.

My cousin Zvi and, until her untimely death, my cousin Ellen and their children live within the greater Boston area. Zvi and I frequently share lunches and the events of our lives. We have a close relationship, and it plays an important role in my life.

Whether as a result of my wartime experiences or simply a personality trait, I have sought stability and continuity and have been reluctant to make major changes in my life. Julie and I celebrated our fiftieth anniversary in December 1998. We have been particularly fortunate in acquiring a close-knit circle of loving friends in our community, truly an extended family. The expectations I had when coming to the United States have come to fruition. Life has been good. I am very content.

Michelson Family Tree

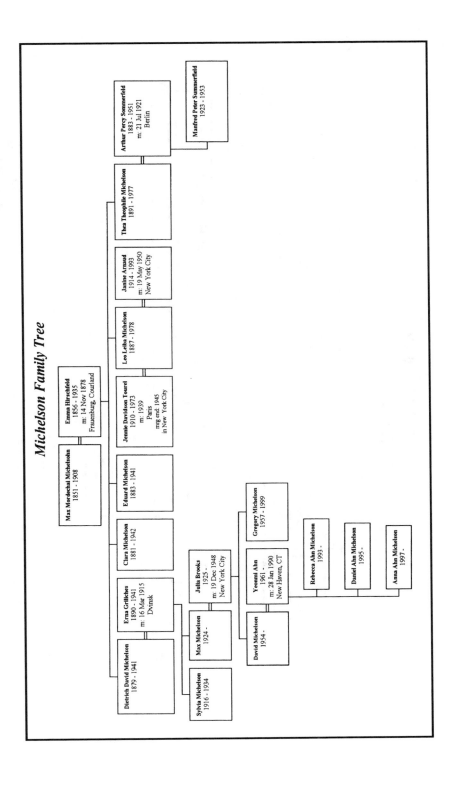

Griliches Family Tree

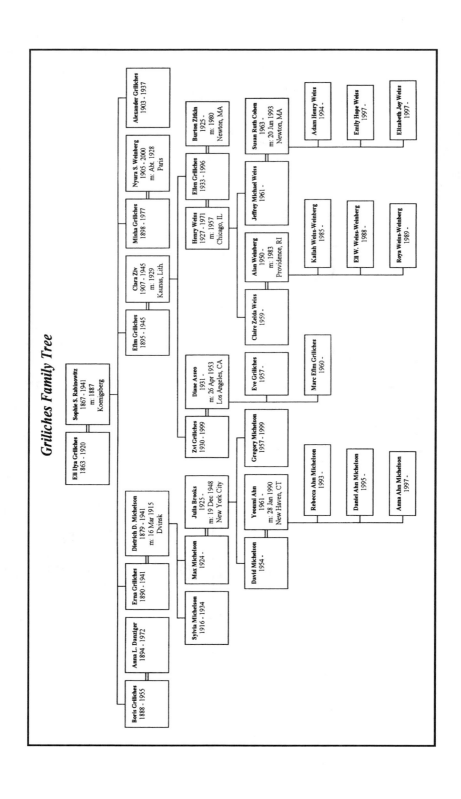

Eli Ibys Griliches
1863 - 1920

Sophie S. Rabinowitz
1867 - 1941
m: 1887
Koenigsberg

Alexander Griliches
1903 - 1937

Nyura S. Weinberg
1905 - 2000
m: Abt. 1928
Paris

Misha Griliches
1898 - 1977

Clara Ziv
1907 - 1945
m: 1929
Kaunas, Lith.

Efim Griliches
1895 - 1945

Burton Zitkin
1925 -
m: 1980
Newton, MA

Ellen Griliches
1933 - 1996

Henry Weiss
1927 - 1971
m: 1957
Chicago, IL

Susan Ruth Cohen
1925 -
m: 20 Jun 1993
Newton, MA

Jeffrey Michael Weiss
1961 -

Adam Henry Weiss
1994 -

Emily Hope Weiss
1997 -

Elizabeth Joy Weiss
1997 -

Alan Weinberg
1950 -
m: 1983
Providence, RI

Claire Zelda Weiss
1959 -

Kailah Weiss-Weinberg
1985 -

Eli W. Weiss-Weinberg
1988 -

Roya Weiss-Weinberg
1989 -

Diane Asseo
1931 -
m: 26 Apr 1953
Los Angeles, CA

Eve Griliches
1957 -

Marc Efim Griliches
1960 -

Zvi Griliches
1930 - 1999

Gregory Michelson
1957 - 1999

Boris Griliches
1888 - 1955

Anna L. Danziger
1894 - 1972

Erna Griliches
1890 - 1941

Dietrich D. Michelson
1879 - 1941
m: 16 Mar 1915
Dvinsk

Julia Brooks
1925 -
m: 19 Dec 1948
New York City

Max Michelson
1924 -

Sylvia Michelson
1916 - 1934

Yeonmi Ahn
1961 -
m: 28 Jan 1990
New Haven, CT

David Michelson
1954 -

Rebecca Ahn Michelson
1993 -

Daniel Ahn Michelson
1995 -

Anna Ahn Michelson
1997 -

Notes

1. *The Jewish Encyclopedia* (New York: Funk and Wagnalls, 1905), Vol. 9, p. 468. See also *Encyclopedia Judaica* (Jerusalem: Macmillan, 1971), Vol. 13, p. 24.
2. Dr. Shaul Lifschitz, "Jewish Communities in Kurland," in Mendel Bobe et al., eds., *The Jews in Latvia* (Tel Aviv: Association of Latvian and Esthonian Jews in Israel, 1971), p. 276.
3. Mendel Bobe, "Four Hundred Years of the Jews in Latvia," in *The Jews in Latvia,* p. 48.
4. Ibid. p. 53.
5. Oscar Handlin, "Introduction," in Simon Dubnov, *History of the Jews* (South Brunswick, NJ: Thomas Yoseloff, 1967), p. 6.
6. Bobe, "Four Hundred Years," p. 84.
7. Anatol Lieven, *The Baltic Revolution* (New Haven: Yale University Press, 1993), p. 142.
8. From a document found in the St. Petersburg archives of the Ministry of the Interior. In April 1909 the congregation submitted a petition to the governor of Livland Province (Liflandskaya Gubernya) requesting permission to transfer the deed to the parcel of land from the three merchants to the congregation.
9. V. N. Latkina, *Uchebnik Istorii Ruskogo Prava* [Textbook of the history of Russian law] (St. Petersburg: Tipografia Montvida, 1909), pp. 180–181.
10. Z. I. Yakub, *Evrei b Daugavpilse* [Jews in Daugavpils] (Daugavpils: Daugavpils Hebrew Society, 1993), p. 40. Translated by the author.
11. Serge Klarsfeld, *Memorial to the Jews Deported From France, 1942–1944* (New York: Beate Klarsfeld Foundation, 1983), pp. 95–101, Transport 11.
12. Bobe, "Four Hundred Years," p. 83.
13. Rainer Esslen, *A Joy to Paint: The Life of Leo Michelson* (Marshall, TX: Michelson Museum of Art, 1998), chapter 9.
14. Bernhard Press, *Judenmord in Lettland* [Murder of Jews in Latvia] (Berlin: Metropol-Verlag, 1992), p. 27.
15. Lieven, *Baltic Revolution,* p. 58.

16. Max Kaufman, *Churbn Lettland, Die Vernichtung der Juden Lettlands* [The destruction of the Jews of Latvia] (München: Self-published, 1947), p. 49.

17. Press, *Judenmord in Lettland,* pp. 58ff.

18. Raul Hilberg, *The Destruction of the European Jews* (New York: Holmes and Meier, 1985), pp. 280ff.

19. Lucy Dawidowicz, *The War Against the Jews* (New York: Bantam, 1975), pp. 279ff.

20. Gertrude Schneider, *Journey Into Terror: The Story of the Riga Ghetto* (New York: Ark House, 1979), pp. 10–11.

21. Hilberg, *Destruction of the European Jews,* pp. 275ff.

22. Ibid., p. 294; also Schneider, *Journey Into Terror,* pp. 10–11.

23. Lieven, *Baltic Revolution,* p. 58.

24. Abraham Shpungin, *Dos is doch geven azey!* [So it was indeed!] (Rehovot, Israel: Self-published, 1991), p. 207.

25. Press, *Judenmord in Lettland,* pp. 70–71.

26. Ibid., p. 74.

27. Hannah Arendt, *Eichmann in Jerusalem* (New York: Penguin, 1977), p. 125.

28. For a discussion of the Arendt-Heidegger relationship, see Elzbieta Ettinger, *Hannah Arendt Martin Heidegger* (New Haven: Yale University Press, 1995).

29. Isaiah Trunk, *Judenrat, the Jewish Councils in Eastern Europe Under Nazi Occupation* (New York: Macmillan, 1978), p. xxxv.

30. Shpungin, *Dos is doch geven azey,* pp. 251–252. Translated by the author.

31. Hilberg, *Destruction of the European Jews,* p. 353.

32. Ibid., pp. 351–352. Also see Schneider, *Journey Into Terror,* pp. 12–13.

33. Press, *Judenmord in Lettland,* p. 128.

34. *New York Times,* March 10, 1965, p. 17. A detailed description of the intelligence operation is given in Anton Künzle and Gad Shimron, *Der Tod des Henkers von Riga* [The death of the hangman of Riga] (Gerlingen: Bleicher, 1999).

35. Kaufman, *Churbn Lettland,* pp. 67–68.

36. Jeanette Wolff, *Mit Bibel und Bebel* (Bonn: Neue Gesellschaft, 1980), pp. 23–24.

37. Schneider, *Journey Into Terror,* p. 21.

38. For a graphic description of life under Kurt Krause, see ibid., chapters 2–4.

39. An authoritative account of these events is given in Israel Kaplan, "Gever in Riger Geto" [Weapons in Riga Ghetto], in Kaplan, ed., *Fun leztn churbn* [From the last destruction], Nos. 1 and 2 (Munich: Central Historical Committee, 1946), pp. 4 and 1, respectively. An abridged translation of the article is found in G. Schneider, ed., *Muted Voices, Jewish Survivors of Latvia Remember* (New York: Philosophical Library, 1987), pp. 29–39. See also Kaufman, *Churbn Lettland,* pp. 196–209; and Press, *Judenmord in Lettland,* pp. 107–112. The accounts differ on some details and dates.

40. Hilberg, *Destruction of the European Jews,* pp. 345–354. See also Schneider, *Journey Into Terror,* p. 23.

41. Lieven, *Baltic Revolution,* p. 148.

42. Agate Nesaule, *A Woman in Amber* (New York: Soho, 1995), pp. 76–79.

43. Kaufman, *Churbn Lettland,* p. 170.

44. Hilberg, *Destruction of the European Jews,* p. 387.

45. Schneider, *Journey Into Terror,* pp. 134–135. See also Wolff, *Mit Bibel und Bebel,* pp. 43–44.

46. Kaufman, *Churbn Lettland,* p. 317.

47. Ibid., p. 319.

48. Tadeusz Skutnik, *Stutthof Historic Guide* (Gdansk: Krajowa Agencja Wydawnicza, 1980), pp. 18–22.

49. Kaufman, *Churbn Lettland,* pp. 490ff.

50. For an account of Lilly's experiences see Lilly Pancis, "Deportation to the East," in G. Schneider, ed., *Muted Voices,* pp. 41–55.

51. Ellen Griliches, "Fun der serie Kinder-Arbeiten: Meine Iberlebungen bet der Milchome" (from the series Children's Works: My Experiences During the War), in *Fun leztn churbn,* No. 9, September 1948, pp. 82–83. Translated by the author.